I KID YOU NOT!

Love
Kang x

LESLEY CREWE

I KID YOU NOT!

• CHRONICLES OF AN ORDINARY FAMILY •

Nimbus Publishing Limited
3660 Strawberry Hill St, Halifax, NS, B3K 5A9
(902) 455-4286 nimbus.ca

Printed and bound in Canada

NB1592

Editor: Penelope Jackson
Editor for the Press: Whitney Moran
Cover and interior design: Jenn Embree

Library and Archives Canada Cataloguing in Publication

Title: I kid you not! : chronicles of an ordinary family / Lesley Crewe.
Other titles: Newspaper columns. Selections
Names: Crewe, Lesley, 1955- author.
Identifiers: Canadiana (print) 20210220945 | Canadiana (ebook) 2021022102X | ISBN 9781774710722 (softcover) | ISBN 9781774710739 (EPUB)
Subjects: LCSH: Crewe, Lesley, 1955-—Anecdotes. | LCSH: Motherhood—Nova Scotia—Cape Breton Island—Anecdotes. | LCSH: Marriage—Nova Scotia—Cape Breton Island—Anecdotes. | LCSH: Families—Nova Scotia—Cape Breton Island—Anecdotes. | LCSH: Cape Breton Island (N.S.)—Biography—Anecdotes. | CSH: Women authors, Canadian (English)—21st century—Anecdotes. | LCGFT: Anecdotes.
Classification: LCC PS8605.R48 A6 2021 | DDC C818/.602—dc23

Nimbus Publishing acknowledges the financial support for its publishing activities from the Government of Canada, the Canada Council for the Arts, and from the Province of Nova Scotia. We are pleased to work in partnership with the Province of Nova Scotia to develop and promote our creative industries for the benefit of all Nova Scotians.

FOR MY GRANDDAUGHTER, GIA ELIZABETH,
A LITTLE SOUL WHO ARRIVED IN 2020,
A BEAUTIFUL SHINING LIGHT IN A DARK WORLD.

CONTENTS

INTRODUCTION

"**/**"

"**C**AN WE ZOOM?"

"You're on mute. I said, you're on mute! It's the button on the left. *The left. The bottom of the screen!* Oh, hell's bells."

"We're in our bubble."

"I'd like to order ten extra-large pizzas."

"I'd like to order ten extra-large pairs of pyjamas."

"I've watched everything on Netflix. Now what?"

The world has become a very different and uncertain place since we first heard the word *COVID-19*. None of us will ever forget the year 2020—or 2021 for that matter—and I don't pretend to know what's going to happen in the future. Our society has been smacked upside the head, and at times it seems too overwhelming to even talk about. But we've also had our heart-warming moments. The realization that we need people and they need us. The one thing we missed the most was each other. Now we know that to hug someone we love is all we want. Nothing else matters.

One of my enduring memories of the first days when we were told to stay home is of watching videos of Italians serenading their neighbours from tiny balconies, with voices and musical instruments. Trying to keep each other company, saying, "You are not alone. We're here too."

Some of these ramblings are about 2020, but not endlessly. It's nicer to remember all the silly stuff that goes on in our lives. But that's a lot easier for me to do, since I live in a part of the world where the tradition of selfless-ness is paramount. We might grumble, but we do our best for one another.

A spoonful of kindness can not only be comforting, but life-saving in times like these.

In the chaotic spirit of the last couple of years, these jottings are in no particular order. They are messy, like life. You can't put memories in a category. Just pick one up, read it, and then toss it on the bedside table. The next entry will be something totally different.

Some of them are from a long time ago, and a good portion are columns I wrote in my final year with *The Chronicle Herald*. I decided to go back to writing novels after that, and *The Spoon Stealer* was born, and now *Nosy Parker*, coming soon. My musings about being a grandmother and living through a pandemic are observations I wrote on my Facebook page or in my private diary.

So enjoy this collection. The years are mixed up, my attitudes change over time, I'm young, I'm old, I'm everything all at once.

I like that.

BECOMING A WRITER

“ **❕** ”

I'VE ALWAYS LOVED FRAN LEBOWITZ.

She's only five years older than I am, so I feel like I've grown up with her. She's been on my radar for fifty years. To me she represents someone who says what's on her mind and doesn't care if people don't like her.

She's worn the same outfit for fifty years, the same look, the same hair, the same glasses. She is who she is and makes no apologies for it. Fran is a famous, grumpy New Yorker who always makes me laugh. She's smart and funny and doesn't own a cellphone or a computer or a microwave. Our lives are the exact opposite and I'm sure she'd ignore me if we ever met and not be my friend, but I've always loved her anyway.

And the fact that one of her best friends was Toni Morrison tells me everything I need to know about Fran.

I'd like to be her. I know I can't, but we admire people whose qualities we find attractive. She's caustic, she smokes, she doesn't cook. She says she's lazy. What's not to admire?

She writes about her world. New York. Makes me want to go there.

I've always loved Rona Maynard.

Since I was old enough to read my mother's *Chatelaine* magazine, I would read Rona's editorial first. She always seemed so knowledgeable. And now that we are friends on Facebook, which thrills me to no end, I read her fascinating posts about art, music, politics, and culture. When you finish reading a link she's sent, you come away enlightened or encouraged, or outraged, or thoughtful.

3

She and her mask and her dog travel throughout her neighbourhood daily and she documents the journey. She writes about her world. Toronto. Makes me want to go there.

I've always loved Lucy Maud Montgomery.

Reading her books throughout my girlhood made me feel like I belonged to her. She and I and Anne were kindred spirits. We loved the same things; we felt the same hurts. We had the same heart. She made me see that the beauty of the natural world and the creatures in it are to be treasured. And family and friends make life worth living. When Matthew died, I cried for days.

She wrote about her world. Prince Edward Island. Makes me want to go there.

These women made me want to write.

So now I write about my world. Cape Breton. Makes me want to go there.

Happily, I made it.

MY BABY BLUEBERRY

"!"

IT DIDN'T START OUT WELL, BUT NOW I KNOW WHY. IT WAS JANUARY 19, IN THE YEAR 2020. Mind you, we didn't know about 2020 in January, and so had no immediate concern. Our first grandchild was due on the 24th. First babies are always late. We'd be going up to Halifax in a couple of days. We didn't want to crowd the poor kids, but of course that's exactly what we were doing. Although they did ask us to come.

And then on the 19th the phone rang in the morning. "We're heading to the hospital."

"You can't be!! I'm not there!"

"Sorry, Mom," Paul said. "Gotta go!"

"JOHNNNNNNNN!!!!! We have to drive to Halifax this minute!!"

He came into the kitchen. "It's a blizzard out there! We can't drive!"

Ignoring him, I shouted, "We're driving and that's that! I will not miss this baby's birth!"

"And I don't want to have an accident on the road. That would be a great gift for the kids and the baby. Dead grandparents."

"You're so mean!" I was hysterical at this point. "I'm flying!"

After spending a fortune on a ticket for myself, I made hubby drive me through a blizzard to the airport because there was no stopping me. We sat there for three hours waiting for the plane to come in, and of course it didn't, because there was a blizzard. We had to drive home in seven feet of snow, me crying the entire way, while hubby cursed the gods as he tried to find the road in blowing snowdrifts.

Gia Elizabeth was born that evening and I was still crying, from happiness, frustration, exhaustion, and wonderment. The first picture arrived. Hubby and I looked at the cellphone in amazement at this precious little bundle of Korean/Scottish/English genes. She was this perfect little doll with her dark hair and big blueberry eyes.

And then, because it was 2020, we lost our power at that exact moment. No internet, no lights, no video chat with our new little family.

I managed to fly out the next day. Poor Grandàd ended up staying away for more than two weeks because of a miserable cough. Gia's auntie Sarah picked me up at the airport, and we hugged each other tight before she drove me to the IWK.

Standing in the hospital hallway, I took a deep breath before entering the room. This was a moment I'd waited for my entire life, and it was unbelievable that it was finally happening. I tiptoed in and there she was in a small cot, all wrapped up in a flannel blanket with a white cap keeping her little head warm.

My son put Gia in my arms and our lifelong love affair began.

And then a scant seven weeks later, the pandemic reared its ugly mug and we didn't see her again in person for months.

In Korea they have a one-hundred-day celebration for baby, called Baek-il. We couldn't go, naturally, but the kids got all gussied up, put Gia in a beautiful dress, and made the special traditional Korean dishes to go with it. Just the three of them instead of a houseful of guests. We watched over a Zoom call and I was so proud.

Of course, I blubbered when the call was done. I'd waited sixty-five years to become a grandmother and longed to spend time with my little muffin.

But everyone in the world was feeling this longing, so I wasn't alone. It just felt like it most of the time.

All the grandmothers I have ever talked to have mentioned how your heart seems to grow three sizes the day your grandchild is born and I'd nod politely and say, "Yes, I'm sure." But I never imagined the depth of the connection.

They finally came to Cape Breton in August and we took her to our beach, and she fell asleep in my arms on a sunny, bright day, with the water shining like diamonds across the sand. She'd snuggled into my neck, wrapped in the hooded beach towel I bought for her, her soft breath against my skin.

My heaven was on a beach chair.

Now I gaze at this delightful, drooling little face playing peek-a-boo with me over the internet, her button nose and eyes scrunching up as she grins with her two bottom teeth peeking out like little pearls.

In spite of what's going on in the world at the moment, everything now makes perfect sense to me.

Because she's here.

2020

“ ❘ ”

ALL OF US DID THE SAME THING IN THE YEAR 2020.
NOTHING!!!

Because of COVID-19, we stayed the blazes home and stared: in the mirror as our hair turned grey; at our loved ones, while we tried to figure out why we loved them; in our suddenly very small houses; at ourselves, as we stretched our stretch pants to the limit; at the television while we watched Netflix to drown out another television screaming American election news.

All of us coping with things we've never had to worry about before.

"Does my mask go with this outfit?"

The panic to buy masks was real, and now I have so many, they're cluttering up the car's glove compartment, my top bureau drawer, the washing machine, the basket by the side door, my purse, and my jacket pockets. No need for a three-layer mask; just wear three.

Remember the early days? Overnight, toilet paper, hand sanitizer, Fleischmann's Yeast, flour, and pressure-treated lumber were like gold, and dealers could be found in dark alleys muttering, "Psst," opening their coats and tossing their heads at you. "Wanna buy some rubbing alcohol?"

I wonder if people are still baking sourdough bread.

In the early days of the pandemic, going to the grocery store was like being in Churchill's War Rooms. Lists, maps, gloves, walkie-talkies, Purell, scrubbed grocery bags, balaclavas. Only one of you could go in, so your better half stayed in the car in case germ warfare got out of hand. When you got home you disinfected the canned tomatoes, turnips, and your entire

9

body with sanitizing Lysol spray. Then cleaned the doorknobs and washed your hands while singing ten rounds of "Happy Birthday," just to be on the safe side.

I'm not quite as paranoid now, but I always remember to put on my mask before I leave the car to do the shopping. Now if only I could remember to take the grocery bags.

But it seems there are always those who don't read the memos. My poor daughter and son-in-law were standing in a lineup when the guy behind them whipped off his mask to have a gigantic sneeze! Eww. What is a mask for? They hightailed it outta there.

It's a sad fact that I'd rather have someone fart in my general direction than have them cough or sniff beside me.

NEOWISE

"!"

S O, HUBBY HAS BEEN OBSESSED WITH THIS NEOWISE COMET THAT HAS BEEN HANGING around for the last week or so. He's been determined to see it.

Looking up at the night sky is a lovely thing to do, until my neck gets sore and I start to get dizzy for some reason.

"Let's go down to the field at the bungalow. We can see the Big Dipper really well from there." Apparently NEOWISE is lurking below the pot part of the Big Dipper.

We arrive too early and have to wait for the sky to really darken up. And it does, everywhere but where we are looking. I'm getting impatient. And standing at night in the middle of a field with not a breath of wind is a stupid thing to do. The mosquitoes can't believe their luck.

We see the space station go by, which is always cool. And remember the old days, if you saw a satellite in the night sky you were really excited. It's a four-lane highway up there now. They are everywhere. That makes me even grumpier.

Finally, I think I see the comet out of the corner of my eye and tell John.

"Are you sure?"

"Yes."

"You're just saying that so we can go."

I don't respond to these kinds of statements anymore.

Then he sees it. So suddenly, it must be there. But it's not a great showing, because there is a layer of clouds lurking about.

Two nights later, I'm in bed reading a book and he pops in the door. "I'm going to the cottage to see the comet. Are you coming?"

"Does it look like I'm coming?"

"You'll be sorry." Off he goes.

Ten more minutes of reading and my eyes are closing, so I turn off the light and go to sleep.

"ARE YOU ASLEEP?!" he hisses.

I look around in a dazed stupor. "Not now! What time is it?"

"After eleven. You can see it from the front deck with binoculars."

"Why did you wake me up?"

"You said you were awake."

I don't respond to these kinds of statements anymore.

As I stagger to the front deck, he puts binoculars in my hand. "You see the big fir tree?"

"No. It's night. It's dark. And there are twenty thousand fir trees in my line of vision."

"Do you see that hole between the trees? One of the trees is bent over and the other one has a wonky branch?"

Just say yes, to get him to stop talking.

"Point the binoculars there."

I look through the binoculars. It's pitch black. No stars. No trees. No comet.

"Do you see it?"

"No."

"You're not pointing it in the right direction."

"John. I don't have my glasses on because I can't see through binoculars with them, and I have ointment in my eyes because of my dry-eye situation. Unless this comet rolls up and parks in the driveway, I can't see it. I'm going to bed."

And I do go to bed. Fifteen minutes later I hear him hurrying down the hallway. "You can see the comet from the highway without binoculars!!"

Graciously, I throw back the covers and stomp out of the house in my nightgown and march up to Highway 255 and stand in the middle of the road, waiting for a car to, please God, hit me and put me out of my misery.

"Do you see it?"

"Yes! I see it."

Now, he's happy as a clam. And we watch it for at least ten minutes, marvelling at the spectacle.

Finally, I march back to bed, and I can't get to sleep because John is snoring. I might forgive him by the time the comet comes around again in six thousand years.

MIND YOUR BUSINESS

"**/**"

YOU GET REALLY NOSY WHEN YOU GET OLDER. I REMEMBER MY GRANDMOTHER, HER sister, and her friend popping up from their chairs in Dora's bungalow to look out the window if a car drove by. Which might have made some kind of sense if it was during the day, but they continued this behaviour at night, as they watched *Maddox* and *Hawaii 5-0*. The three heads would appear like gophers out of a hole, and then disappear again, to discuss who it might have been out at this ungodly hour. Anyone out after nine o'clock at night was just asking for trouble.

Yesterday, while bobbing in the ocean with two friends, all of us six feet apart, we noticed someone walking down the beach.

"Who's that coming? Is that Linda?"

"No, I don't think so. She's moving too fast."

"Must be Patricia or Wanda. They're tall."

"There's a guy behind her. Is that Pat?"

"No, he's limping."

"Oh, must be John."

"No, I believe it's Lloyd. Doesn't he have a bum right knee?"

"No, his limp is on the left."

"And it's not his knee, it's his hip."

The fact that we don't bother to wait until this person is close enough to identify shows you that it doesn't take much to amuse us during these pandemic days.

And I definitely sounded like my grandmother when I came across a stunning young woman lying on the sand far enough away from my beach chair. "Hi, sweetheart. Who do you belong to?"

"I'm Sam. Shirley Scott's granddaughter."

"Land sakes! I remember the day you were born! I remember the day your mother was born! Why, I remember when your grandmother brought your mother to the bungalow for the first time and a flying squirrel got in through the window…"

Sam patiently gives me a sweet smile, as youngsters do when you're boring them to death with stuff they don't need to know.

And now that I'm a grandmother I'm like a coiled spring, ready to go off at any moment if someone asks me about my little Gia. The words don't even make it out of their mouths before I'm fumbling in my beach bag for my phone.

"Oh! My little blueberry!!!! She's so, so, so, so, so, so, so, so—"

"Cute?"

"How did you guess?!"

Have you ever tried to see a picture on a cellphone at the beach in the glaring sun? It can't be done. That never stops a really determined grandmother. But now I can't hold the phone close enough for them to try and take a peek, and I don't want other people to hold it, so they have to squint and say "Awww" before they quickly give up and go back to putting on sunscreen.

Then I asked Rebecca and Jill about their ceremony planned for next year.

"How many people have you invited?"

(This is none of my business, by the way.)

"150."

"WHATTTT???"

"We both have large families. But who knows? Plans may change."

They shouldn't have to explain this to me, because again, it's none of my business. But since I'm old and nosy now, instead of saying, "How lovely," whether they are inviting two people or two thousand, I give them my opinion, which they never asked for. And I really don't have an opinion, except when you say "WHATTTT?" to something, it certainly sounds like you do.

This is what old people do. I am definitely my mother and grandmother rolled into a big bag of wind.

But there is a part of me that is enjoying this. I've lived long enough to be really annoying.

It's like having a Get Out of Jail Free card.

ROUND ISLAND GIRL

"**/**"

GROWING UP IN THE BIG CITY OF MONTREAL WAS EXCITING. WE HUNG AROUND WITH a bunch of kids of every nationality. We played in back alleys, ran along concrete sidewalks, and biked beside busy streets. We loved it. But when the hot days of summer came, there was no place on earth we wanted to be more than our bungalow in Round Island, Cape Breton.

My sister and I would make ourselves sick with anticipation, and inevitably one or both of us would come down with mumps or strep throat the night before we left. Into the back seat of the car we would go, along with the dog, the two cats, and endless luggage. Cars were like boats back then. They held everything.

The excitement would begin when we neared the Causeway. We'd start to hoot and holler: just two more hours in a stifling hot and furry car. At the end of Hornes Road, we'd roll down the windows and breathe in the glorious and cool salty breeze. The dog was frantic by now. Turning down the lane and finally being set free, we'd tumble over each other in our haste to be the first one to run to the beach, just to make sure it was still there.

Thus began our endless summer. Summer lasted forever back then. Heck, one day lasted forever. We lived in our bathing suits and never wore shoes. We had one towel each that only got washed when it was caught in a downpour on the clothesline. Our days were spent with the gang, draped over bunk beds and old sofas reading Archie comics and chewing bubble gum.

Then someone would yell "Let's go to the beach!" and we'd tear off, banging the screen door, chasing each other through the path in the woods and over hot, spiky blades of grass in the field, then hurling ourselves into the ice-cold water. There we would stay for the entire day, splashing, diving, and pushing each other around until someone's mother would yell at the lot of us to "get home now if you want any supper."

We never cared what we looked like. No one brushed their hair. Not that you could get a brush through it anyway, it was so encrusted with salt. Our feet were black and our heels were like cement. We were as brown as berries. One year some of the older girls told me if you put lemon juice in your hair it would turn blonde. I picked pulp out of my scalp for weeks.

Every night after supper our motley crew would gather in Scott's field to play baseball until dark and then walk each other home, scaring ourselves sick over the Round Island Terror, a ghost story that came in handy when you wanted to grab on to whoever you had a crush on that summer.

On rainy days we would gather together to play Rummoli or Racko, or read old Harlequin romances that gathered dust in the corner. We'd make fudge and chow down on endless boxes of Kraft dinner.

We would go for picnics and gather seashells. Our grandmothers would make us pick berries in the field on hot August afternoons. Poor Grammy would always tsk when I offered my plastic shortening container full of leaves, branches, and bugs mixed with a few blueberries.

Thelma always kept great tubs of ice cream in her freezer, so we would run to her place and get an ice cream cone for a dime. Then we would race up to the tree house and eat to our hearts' content. It always tasted better up there.

The stars at night are what I remember most. Lying in the field at night, listening to the adults sing old songs by the bonfire. Looking up and feeling so small in the face of such splendour. The night would wrap me up in its arms and I would feel safe in my small Round Island world.

Now I take my own children to this place. But alas, I am the adult and have to do stuff like drag things to the beach and set up housekeeping, with coolers and umbrellas, hats, T-shirts, and sunblock. We have boats and water-skis, noodles and floats. Now I feed people and count heads.

But then it happens. My kids race back into the water. Dark shadows against a dazzling summer sun. The water glistens all around them. I squint my eyes and put my hand up to shade my brow. Their laughter is an echo of my sister and me, a long time ago when we were young and free as birds.

WHAT?! WHAT?!

"¡"

OH, FOR THE GOOD OLD DAYS WHEN DRY EYES WERE MY ONLY PROBLEM.
As I walk out of the eye doctor's office, I notice there is a hearing clinic right next door. Immediately, hubby's voice is in my head.

"You never listen! You should get your hearing checked."

Oh, please. We've been married for forty-three years. All wives who've made it to this milestone are happily tuning out their husbands. We have to, or we'll go mad.

Still, I suppose it wouldn't hurt. Hearing tests are fun. They don't require needles, or fasting after midnight, or memorizing stuff. You just sit in a phone booth. It's like an unheated sauna with a big window, where you get to stare at the audiologist and pretend you're Captain Kirk. "Warp speed, Mr. Sulu."

You have to listen and repeat words, let her know if you hear beeping out of one ear or the other, can you hear static or other weird noises? Nothing to do but nod and smile. Gosh, I'm acing this test.

The lovely audiologist, who is young enough to be my daughter (every young woman I meet now qualifies on this score), tells me to watch my step getting out of my little prison, and naturally I trip despite the warning. This is strangely prophetic.

While I smugly sit by her desk, waiting to be released back to my regular day, confident in the knowledge that I am fine, I worry that I've wasted this woman's time. Hope she doesn't mind.

"How did I do?" I grin.

She hesitates. "You have mild to moderately severe hearing loss."

I chuckle. "Get outta here."

"No, really."

Now I stare at her. *"What?! What?!"*

It strikes me funny that I'm yelling these words at a woman who's telling me I can't hear. "That's not possible!"

She shows me the reading. It looks okay in some spots, but then dips downward, resembling a graph of the '29 Wall Street Crash.

"But I can hear you!"

"You're fine face-to-face. It's the higher register that's particularly bad. I know you weren't expecting this. I wasn't expecting this either."

Perhaps the fact that I'm now slumped in my chair gave it away. "So, what does this mean?"

"You need hearing aids in both ears."

"What?! What?! How much is that?"

"From two to six thousand dollars."

"What?!"

When I go home and walk into the kitchen, hubby asks me how it went.

"You were right. I wasn't listening." And then I burst into tears and howl. He hugs me.

"We could be going on a river cruise in Europe. Instead, I'll be sticking two little metal lima beans in my ears."

That night I call the kids because I need to *hear* their voices.

My son mentions that I always turn up the volume on the television. My daughter reminds me of the time we were outside at twilight and she said, "Listen to the peepers." And I couldn't hear them. I'd completely forgotten about that, although it gave me a stab of panic at the time.

And then my wonderful, sensible Korean daughter-in-law says matter-of-factly, "Mother. You will need to hear the baby."

So, that's it. I will wear hearing aids so I can hear my first little grandchild crying, and now it all doesn't seem so bad.

I'm lucky I live in a time where hearing loss can be fixed. I'm lucky I can afford the hearing aids. I'm lucky I'm not profoundly deaf.

But I have to say the last few weeks have been eye-opening. Someone up there wants me to know I've entered a new stage in life. I'm going to be a grandmother. My Old Age Security application is in the mail, my back tooth is falling out of my head ($$$), not to mention getting physio on my bum ankle, and now I need hearing aids. The only thing left to do is let my hair grow grey and my transformation will be complete.

Oh, no. Just realized I'll be hearing everything hubby says, so I really must take up drinking.

WHAT DO I DO NOW?

"I"

THERE'S NO PHRASE THAT STRIKES MORE FEAR IN THE HEARTS OF HUMANKIND THESE days than "The internet's down!"

All life as we know it ceases to exist, and we go into a collective tailspin when we call our internet provider and there's a message that says our area is experiencing difficulties and you'll have to call back for further updates. So, it's serious! It's not something that can be fixed by unplugging and re-plugging some router that's lurking in the back of your credenza in a maze of dusty wires.

If someone asked me if I was online all day, I'd say, "Heavens, no! That's ridiculous." But that goes to show you how delusional I can be, because now that the internet has been down since last night, it has seriously messed up my morning, and I never realized how much of my routine is wrapped around this marvellous technology in the early hours of the day.

What's the first thing I do when I swing my feet from the bed to the floor? Turn on the computer in my study on my way to the bathroom. Then return to type in my password before heading to the kitchen to fill the coffee maker. Out the door for my walk; walk, walk, walk; back to press the coffee on before taking a shower, make poached eggs on toast and head back to my study to sip my coffee while I check my personal and business email and read various newspapers from around the world. Then I go on Facebook to see what my three friends are up to, and accidentally read about the lives of the other six hundred people I've added as friends but who I wouldn't necessarily recognize on the street. But that's okay, because they're delightful and I get a kick out of people's celebrations, trips abroad, and pictures of their grandchildren and dogs.

Then hubby's emails start piling in. He's in his lounger in the living room drinking his coffee with a laptop, not surprisingly, on his lap, and I'm in my study not ten feet from him, but he sends me emails from the Weather Network about various weather disasters, a husky dog meeting his human baby for the first time, cockatoos having a dance-off, cats being cats, meteor showers in the night sky, and whales jumping out of the water.

I can't believe how much I'm missing that this morning.

Well, I have to get down to business, and I need a quote for something I'm working on. I'll google it. Nope. No Google. So, I think about dinner. Maybe baked haddock. What temperature should the oven be? I'll google it. Nope. No Google. Gosh, I must answer that invitation to do a reading in October. Nope. No email. I wonder what day Sarah is driving home with the dog. I'll message her on Hangouts. Nope. Not working.

I've become so used to staring at this computer screen while I drink my morning coffee that I feel like I have a limb missing this morning. And that is a sobering thought. It used to be, years ago, that the first thing I did was grab my coffee and a book off the bedside table and hoe into that for an hour before doing the dishes and getting on with my day. I didn't feel like I was missing anything, and if I wanted news about friends or my kids, I'd call them.

But that doesn't happen anymore as a rule. Now it's messaging or texts. However, I still call the kids because I'm their mother and they're not getting off that easy. These are voices I need to hear.

So, what have I done while my internet has been down this morning? Well, I wrote a column, cleaned the bathroom, vacuumed, made a grocery list, straightened my humidity hair, did my foot exercises, read five chapters of a novel, watered the plants, dusted, made a casserole, and mucked out the freezer.

Based on this experiment, I'd say my life is much more productive without the internet. But I just know that I've missed a fluffy corgi butt sashaying down the sidewalk and a baby elephant plopping into a kiddie pool without me!

And that's just wrong.

CATS OR DOGS?

"I"

WHENEVER I MEET SOMEONE NEW IN A SOCIAL SETTING (WHICH HASN'T OCCURRED in more than a year), I play a little game with myself and wonder if they are cat or dog people.

There are clues you can spot right off the bat.

Dog people obviously have cars with old blankets completely covered in dog fur and mud on the back seat. Cat people are happy to carry cat fur on their clothes.

Cat people have old, sort-of old, and new cat scratches all over their hands and arms. Dog people have enormous pockets filled with poop bags, leashes, doggie treats, and water bottles.

Dog people have back sliding doors covered with wet nose prints, just above your knees.

Cat people have nothing on their windowsills because their cats knocked it all off long ago.

Dog people have learned to keep their wastepaper baskets Kleenex free, or at least buy ones with lids, but that never stops a really determined dog.

Cat people can never keep a glass of water by their bedside. There's always been a cat tongue in there at some point.

Cat people can go an entire day without finding their pet and grow hoarse calling their name before their feline appears, wondering what their problem is.

Dog people always have a slobbery dog underfoot.

Cat people think it's cute when their cats curl up in the bathroom sink and take endless pictures and post them on YouTube.

Dog people shout at their dogs when they jump into the tub to keep their human kid happy. They always have a video of it and post this on YouTube as well.

Dog people put cardboard signs around their pups' necks to shame them. "I ate the pot roast." "I ate the Kleenex in the wastepaper basket."

Cat people don't do this. (See point about cat scratches.)

Dog people let their dogs hang out of car windows.

Cat people keep their cats in jail on car trips.

Cat people think cats are superior because they use a litterbox, like the tidy animals they are.

Dog people think dogs are superior even when they're shitting on everyone's lawns and you have to pick up the shit and take it with you.

There are people out there who don't like cats *or* dogs, but I avoid them, which is unfair, I suppose, but too bad. We have nothing in common.

I am a cat person who adores dogs. I am a dog person who adores cats. I love all animals equally. If I could get away with having a baby hippo in my house, I would.

WALKING

"I"

ALL THE EXPERTS AGREE: WALKING IS A MARVELLOUS WAY TO GET YOURSELF SORTED, physically, mentally, and emotionally. There is nothing better than communing with nature and smelling the fresh air. We have an advantage here in the Maritimes of being able to smell the ocean as well, which is heavenly.

But getting out the door to go for a walk is a challenge. Especially with a retired husband lurking around the joint.

I put on my jacket.

"Where are you going?"

"For a walk."

"Want some company?"

Not really, but if I say this out loud, I'm an itch with a b in front of it. Telling someone no doesn't mean you don't love them, it just means you want some time to yourself. But that's never the way it comes across, no matter how you try to wiggle around it.

"I thought I'd listen to audio affirmations on my earphones. It's part of my strategy for a better me."

"You won't be better. You'll be dead if you wear earphones on the highway. You won't hear the cars. That's not happening."

Good grief. "Fine. But I'm leaving now."

"I'll just be a second."

Oh, come now. They weren't planning on walking until a minute ago, so they aren't ready and now they have to get ready, while you stand by the door in your boots and mitts.

He roars around the house trying to find his "walking socks," pulling on his sweatshirt, taking a detour to the john, grabbing Kleenex, his boots, his walking stick, his special hat, and fumbling through the eighteen pairs of gloves and mitts in the basket by the back door to find the ones he wants. By this time, I'm sweating.

Finally, we're both outdoors in the cold. We live on a gravel laneway, so depending on the weather, this is a dangerous route. Most of the time it's covered in ice, so now I get the running commentary on where I should walk.

He points. "I put down sand. Walk there."

So, I walk there. Now we're at the end of the driveway, both of us still intact.

"Don't walk from here to the mailbox. It's too slippery. Walk on the left side of the laneway."

I want to salute him, but I don't. He'll get annoyed. We start down the left-hand side, but it's not good. We can't build up a sweat shuffling around at a snail's pace.

"We better walk on the highway," he says. "But turn down those earphones."

"What?"

He points at my ears. "TAKE THOSE OUT!"

This time I do salute him. But he's right. You can't take a chance on a highway, even a rural one, so my affirmations stop and go in my pocket.

Now we're on the highway, supposedly walking together. But we have never walked together in our lifetime, because for some reason John has always walked ahead of me. And not just me, everyone. It's like he can't stand having someone at his side. So, I get to look at his back and have the end of his walking stick almost hit me with every stride, because he doesn't use the walking stick, only carries it. It's supposed to be in case a coyote pops out of nowhere, but if that happened, we'd only take a picture.

Now I hurry to catch up. "Walk with me. Just stay right here. Like this. Isn't this nice?"

He smiles and nods and then ever so slowly quickens his pace until he is ahead of me.

"CAR!"

We move to the shoulder of the road and wave at the car going by. Have no idea who's in it, but it's surely a neighbour of some sort.

"SCHOOL BUS!"

Back on the shoulder.

28

When he gets too far ahead, I get annoyed, so I rush to catch up and put out my hand. "Hold my hand. Then maybe you'll stay put."

"You can't hold hands wearing puffy mitts."

"Try it."

We try it. We have no sense of rhythm together. We're as awkward as kids in kindergarten.

I'm the first to let go. "I so envy people who can walk together, holding hands."

"It's stupid."

"No, it's not. It's lovely."

"There's more than one way to show a person you love them."

"Oh yeah?"

"BIG MONSTER TRUCK!" He pulls me off the road and stands in front of me as one of the trucks from the local mine comes charging down the highway. He takes the brunt of the slushy mess that sprays in the air.

He's got a point.

VISITING THE KIDS

"I"

WE LIVE IN CAPE BRETON. OUR CHILDREN LIVE IN HALIFAX. EVERY SO OFTEN WE get sick of our own company and decide we need to hug our kiddies or we'll lose our will to live, so we decide we're going down to give them the pleasure of our company.

Naturally we call them first. Or think we did.

"So, we'll see you on Sunday."

"Oh?"

"We're coming for a week. We told you."

"No, you didn't."

"Are you sure?"

"You never mentioned it, but don't worry. It'll be great to see you." I get off the phone. "I thought you told the kids we were coming."

"I thought you did."

It's a good thing the two of us aren't in charge of anything important.

Three days out, hubby is in full swing, getting every scrap of snow away from our property. The roof is done, the pathway shovelled for the oil man, the backyard immaculate so our neighbour can come and feed our birds, the compost bin uncovered, and the underground drainage pipe for the dry well inspected, in case it's frozen and water backs up when we're gone.

On second thought, hubby could run the country.

Forty-eight hours before we leave, I start washing all our clothes, even though my children do have their own washers and dryers. It's just not the same. Then small pockets of stuff start appearing in the hallway, bathroom, bedroom, spare room, and kitchen.

Hubby trips over one of the mounds. "Does this have to be here?"

"If I don't pile up things when I think of them, I'll forget them. This is writer stuff, this is cat stuff, this is a bag of running shoes, and this contains a hairdryer, a straightener, and a curling iron."

But it's okay for him to drag the world's biggest cooler up the stairs.

"What do we need that for?"

"I might want to bring a sandwich."

"We can buy a sandwich on the way."

"I have to go to Costco and buy more Balderson aged cheddar."

It's true. It's the highlight of his visit to Halifax, although I doubt the cheese would go bad without refrigeration in the five hours it takes to drive home, but try telling him that.

Speaking of food, twenty-four hours before we depart, we start cleaning out the fridge of things that may grow fuzz while we're gone. Before every trip our dinners usually consist of leftover chicken noodle soup, four strips of bacon, a side order of peas, ham slices, a tomato, and white bread crusts. Dessert is always three soft oranges.

"Why don't you make banana muffins with these ripe bananas?" he suggests.

Why don't I throw them in the compost bin because I have enough to do? But my guilt will kick in and the stupid muffins will be made.

On this trip I have four writer events to attend, which means I'm in a dither about what boots to bring. I can't wear what I usually wear around here, because I'm going to run into people in the city, and that doesn't happen often in my neighbourhood. My old crappy grey boots are fine for coyotes, but not for conducting a workshop with actual human beings.

I do some deep breathing, but that solves nothing, so I'll have to go shopping in Halifax.

The morning of our departure, the suitcases are bulging, our toiletry bags are stuffed, and another cloth bag is recruited for all our pill bottles and vitamins. The cat's carrier, blanket, favourite stuffed toy, cat dishes, and litterbox are pristine and ready to go. We just have to endure the drama of getting Pip in the carrier without having our faces ripped to shreds. Pip is grumpy in his old age.

The last rites are checking for spare keys, water bottles, sunglasses, wallets, and the cellphone.

We get in the car and look at each other.

"Have we got everything?"

I nod. "There's not a darn thing left in the house worth taking."

So, off we go to the big city, to see our most prized possessions.

THIS OLD TREE

" | "

W E HAVE A DEAD TREE IN OUR BACKYARD THAT IS COMPLETELY STRIPPED OF ITS bark, so basically it looks like a piece of vertical driftwood rising forty feet in the air. To look at it, you'd think it had no purpose, but nothing could be farther from the truth. Its stark beauty fascinates me, especially against a moonlit night sky.

We call it the crow tree, because this is where our thirty to forty crows gather every day for their breakfast and afternoon snacks. Over the years, their preening beaks and sharp claws have shaved away what little bark there was, and now all that's left is smooth, white wood.

The curved branches are outstretched like welcoming arms, and at least five crows can roost quite happily on each one. There are ten floors in all, but near the top, the branches have only enough room for a single occupant. The sentinel, as we call him, always sits at the very top, like a Christmas star. It's his job to let the others know when John rounds the corner with his bucket of goodies. When the sentinel starts squawking, you can watch the crows glide in from the four corners of their estate.

It's only after hubby comes back into the house that the crows nestle into the tree branches, and this is where their complicated ballet recital starts. The food is left on top of the cover of my dad's old trailer, so it really does resemble an outdoor dining room table. One of the lower branches is only a few feet away from the feast. This is the most prized spot on the tree, and I've noticed that only the big boys get to sit here, or maybe it's just my feverish imagination, because let's face it, crows all look alike.

Some sort of secret signal is then given, and all the crows descend on the trailer at once, to peck away for about three seconds before instantly rising into the tree branches again. What spooked them? Nothing that I can see. They do this at least sixty times in the five minutes it takes to polish up all the grub. Flutter, rise. Flutter, fall. Those who can't find space on the branches hover back down to the ground. Some rebellious types skip the yo-yoing performance and walk with a haughty attitude under the bird feeders and peck away at the odd sunflower seed.

I honestly think if we ever got rid of this tree, we wouldn't have this daily ritual. Maybe a few crows, but not this entire community, who have learned that they can gather safely within these branches while they have their morning meal.

You'd think a dead thing would have no purpose, but our crow tree is a daily reminder that even when you think something is over, it doesn't have to be. I'm positive that when this tree was young and beautiful, it never got nearly the number of visitors than it does now.

This gives me hope, for some reason.

If we were to ever sell this property, I can guarantee the crow tree would be the first thing people would notice and shake their heads at. "Who wants an old dead tree in the backyard? Cut it down!"

Luckily, we have a loyal committee of squawky feathered neighbours who could show up in an instant and put on a very animated rendition of Alfred Hitchcock's movie *The Birds*.

And that, as they say, would be that.

THINGS YOU SHOULD NEVER DO WITH YOUR HUSBAND

"|"

THERE ARE SOME THINGS YOU SHOULD NEVER DO WITH YOUR HUSBAND. LIKE TAKE him to see the movie *The Favourite*.

What was I thinking? *The Favourite* is clearly an artsy, avant-garde film that can only truly be appreciated by film buffs and people who are keen to see Olivia Coleman in action. People who love cinematography and set design. People like me.

Not someone who thinks *Blazing Saddles* is the best film ever made.

When a dance sequence comes on the screen. I make the mistake of turning my head to glance at him. He rolls his eyes so spectacularly, I can see it in the darkened theatre. He leans over. "Who dances like that?"

"SHHHH! You don't take it literally! This is poetic license!"

"This is crap."

Fortunately, we are the only ones in the back row, so we don't disturb the general public.

But now that I know he's less than thrilled with this movie, I'm on edge. Yes, it's over the top, but I like that...the performances, the mood, the lighting, the things not said.

He leans over again. "Why are they throwing fruit at that naked guy?"

"SHHHH!"

There's an image that involves leg-rubbing and a kaleidoscope of rabbits before it fades to black. Hubby stares at me with incredulity when the lights go up.

"That's it? What the heck was that supposed to mean?"

"The futility of it all."

"Oh, spare me. Did you actually like it?"

"Yes! I did. Or at least I was enjoying it until you broke the spell."

"What spell?"

"John, I go to the movies to get away from real life. I want to be transported to another world, not sit mired in this one with you moaning about it."

We head to the parking lot. He points at me. "*Young Frankenstein*. Now, that was a good movie."

This is why I normally go alone to a movie theatre. Who needs the aggravation of someone else's opinion?

There's something else I don't like doing when hubby is with me. Trying to pick out a greeting card. He stands there looking at his watch.

"Just pick one."

"I can't take the first one I see."

He reaches over and takes one out of the slot. "Here's Snoopy. He's perfect for every occasion."

"Not when you're sending a sympathy card."

"Who died?"

"No one. It's Valentine's Day. I want to send the kids something."

"They like Snoopy."

"Leave me alone for five minutes."

He wanders off, but I know he's around and that makes me nervous. When I'm in front of a card display, I like looking at everything, and that takes a while. Hubby thinks it's a huge waste of time.

He wanders back. "Find anything?"

"Not yet."

"Are they sending you a Valentine's Day card?"

"What difference does that make? I'm not doing it to get a card back. I'm doing it for myself. It makes me feel good."

"You're a writer. Just write something and send that. You'll save yourself fifteen bucks."

"How about I write, 'Dear kids, your father doesn't want to send you a card, so I guess he doesn't love you as much as I do'?"

"Sounds great. Let's go."

And lastly, don't ever try to clean out the basement if your husband is within five hundred miles of you, because he will instantly appear out of nowhere and root through any garbage bags you've accumulated.

"Are you crazy? You can't throw away that old tobacco tin full of rusty washers. They come in handy."

"There were cobwebs all over it. How handy can they be?"

"You never know. And don't throw out those towels. They make great rags."

"We have six boxes of great rags that I found under another blanket of cobwebs. You have to get rid of some of this stuff!"

"Why don't I get rid of you?" he replies.

"That sounds like a wonderful plan."

JUNKIE

"I"

B ECAUSE I CAN'T CONCENTRATE DURING THIS QUARANTINE, I'M NOT WRITING OR reading. Hubby and I aren't making dance videos to cheer people up, as our efforts would have the opposite effect. My housework regime is still in neutral, where it's always been, and I'm not joining recipe exchanges online because that smacks of work.

A great inertia has descended over my body, and now I plunk my arse in front of the television, my computer, and my tablet to watch endless TV series and movies, so I can forget the fact that I can't be with our new little granddaughter, who is of course the world's most beautiful child.

But I've come to realize that there is no rhyme or reason for the choices I'm making. I'm all over the map, like a crazed Peter Rabbit in Mr. McGregor's garden.

A friend has bugged me for a couple of years to watch *Ozark*.

"I don't want to watch crap about money laundering with the cartel."

Because of this isolation, I finally relented. My God! Every single day in the Byrde household would give me a full-blown heart attack. And yet I watched all three seasons, just to hear Ruth curse.

Then I went bananas for Icelandic murder mysteries. Subtitles are not ideal for remembering the names of murder suspects and good guys, unless the name is Sven. I fell in love with the police chief in *Trapped*! A huge teddy bear of a man. Yummy.

I'm watching every British murder mystery out there. (Murder seems to be on my mind at the moment.) And all the English actors I love are in every one of them. There must be only one hundred actors in Britain and they recycle them endlessly, but who cares? They're fabulous.

We watched five seasons of *Line of Duty*. Now I want to be a British D. I. when I grow up.

Started to watch the series *Scandal*, only because it said it had seven seasons, and since we'll be in lockdown until Christmas, I thought it would pass the time. I'm unsure of Olivia Pope. She can talk the hind leg off a donkey and reduce grown men to tears with her tongue. It's like a superpower.

At night in bed, I watch *Fleabag* with earphones on, because I love a good giggle and I always feel like I'm watching something I shouldn't, because I'm supposedly a matron now, but Fleabag is my hero.

Then it's time for Heidi Klum and Tim Gunn to rip designers to shreds with pinking shears! I'm on pins and needles with every episode to see who gets lambasted.

At some point, this is going to have to end, because now I really want to go to Iceland and Norway and Finland and England and Wales and the Shetland Islands, thanks to these detective shows, but we're not allowed to leave the house. It's so depressing.

But I'm not going to the Ozarks. They're mad as hatters down there.

WRAP IT UP!

"**!**"

*C*RAFTY IS NOT MY MIDDLE NAME.

It would be nice to possess this amazing gene, but alas, it's not to be. That doesn't mean I haven't attempted a few things over the years. Once I did learn to knit ski socks, but gave up when the cat got into the ones I'd intended for my father. She pulled the wool all over the living room. The quilt I made for my sister's wedding was so traumatizing, I never did it again. Then there was rug hooking for a while, but there's only so much floor space available in my house for slippery rugs. Crocheting defeated me outright because the throw turned out to be a diamond shape instead of a square.

Jealousy rears its ugly head when I see people wrapping gifts beautifully. It doesn't even matter what the gift is. The wrapping is perfect, because they put things in baskets, or Mason jars, or handmade plates with doilies. Their ribbons are full and tight, their paper is thick and colourful. Even their handwriting is astonishing. They make potato prints with powered paint and stamp brown paper in a pattern. They use comic strips and glitter with pine cones and put coloured pins in Styrofoam balls! Popcorn and candy canes fill takeout boxes, and fresh cookies are wrapped in Cellophane with raffia and cinnamon sticks!!

How the hell do these people do it?

But I've realized one thing. These crafty sorts must be incredibly patient people. And they must own heavy-duty glue guns. They have to know their way around craft stores too. This is my downfall. Wandering around aisles filled with small paper stars and felt animal shapes is one thing, but to actually reach out and take something off the hook would mean I know what I'm going to make, and my mind goes blank in that instant. There might be something better down another aisle, and then what would I do with this neon pad of sticky paper?

So as a consequence, I really, really hate wrapping Christmas gifts, because I know I'm lousy at it. But I didn't realize I had a reputation for being a bad wrapper until my nieces and kids were talking about Christmas one summer and Jessica piped up, "Oh, we always knew which ones Auntie Lelly wrapped. They were usually torn, with really cheap paper and the stick-on bow would be falling off!" They had a huge laugh over that.

Look, I could buy more expensive paper, but every year I see the seven-dollar package with eight rolls of paper and grab it. Same thing with the Christmas cards. Cheapo is the theme, so my holiday cards usually have penguins falling on ice or a bear carrying a tree. I just don't want to spend a fortune on Christmas paper—it's only going to be ripped off in two seconds flat!

One Christmas I made the mistake of saying that I was going to put the presents in store-bought gift bags. They looked at me like I was mad.

"No way! That's no fun!"

It was the same reaction when I mentioned having a Christmas ham instead of turkey.

"Never!" "You wouldn't!" "How could you?"

Because I dislike this chore so much, I do my best to get myself in the spirit, by putting on the fireplace channel and listening to Christmas music. This gets me through the first hour. But after that, my back starts to hurt and my wrists are sore. With each gift, I get sloppier and sloppier. If I have a foot of paper on either side of the box, I fold it up anyway and tape the bulges that are sticking out. Since no one gives you gift boxes anymore, I'm wrapping things that are odd shapes. How do you wrap a ball cap and have it look good? It can't be done.

By the time I'm finished, I hate my kids, I hate my husband, I hate our cats, I hate my son's cat and my daughter's dog. They can all get stuffed! Will I get any credit for doing this odious chore? Not likely.

Oh yeah, and on top of that my daughter and daughter-in-law have birthdays in December, so I have to wrap up their gifts as well.

The Grinch and I have a lot in common.

WRAP IT UP, GRANDMOTHER EDITION

"!"

S0, I WROTE THAT LAST WRAP IT UP COLUMN A HUNDRED YEARS AGO. Now I'm a baby girl's grandmother, and I've had to rethink this crafty business. One thing that hasn't changed is my hatred for craft projects, but it's not about me anymore, is it?

A thought went through my head that this was Gia's first Christmas and I had to make her something. My kids have always loved the red burlap Advent calendar my sister made for them forty years ago. We still use it to this day.

AHA! I'll make one for Gia and her parents, and I'll make one for my daughter, Sarah, and her husband since they love Christmas.

What in Sam Hill was I thinking?

To say I agonized over these damn things for three months is not an exaggeration, and I started shopping in places I've rarely been in, like Michaels. It's another world in that joint. And this was when all the Halloween decorations were still up and I was looking for Santa baby and all things Christmassy.

Red burlap was nowhere to be found, so I bought a natural colour but sparkly. I had to make do with white Velcro instead of red, and I bought enough sticky-backed felt to cover a football field but realized too late I only needed the regular stuff. There is now a huge bag of sequins, little pom-pom

45

balls, stars, glitter, bottles of glue and yarn stuffed in a drawer, howling to get out.

And then I remembered I had to cut out all the numbers by hand. Twenty-six number ones. Sixteen number twos, etc. etc. And worst of all, I needed a sewing machine to make twenty-four pockets on one calendar and twenty-four pockets on the other one.

I don't own a sewing machine.

Instantly I called my neighbour, Yvonne Kennedy, who is the quintessential craft expert in our neck of the woods.

"I'm doing a project with burlap and felt."

You'd have to know Yvonne. She gave me her high-pitched scream and howled with laughter. "YOU?! Are you crazy?"

"I just need some advice."

"You want me to do it."

"No." *YES*. "I'm just going to bring it down and you can advise me."

She took one look at it and told me what to do, then looked at my face and grabbed the bag out of my hand. "Jesus, Jesus. I'll do it."

"It's only a few straight lines sewn. I have to do everything else."

"You better believe it."

She brought it back two days later. "There is no way in hell you would've been able to do this. It was the wrong burlap and kept shredding, so I've sewn up all the seams with edging."

They looked so good I thanked her over and over again and wanted to hug her, but because of COVID-19 I didn't, so I gave her a signed copy of my new novel instead.

Then I spent two more weeks gathering up small Christmas items to use as tokens for each pocket. Can I just say, I hate glue guns?

Next, I painted a small rocking chair I had in the house, and hooked a rug mat for the seat. A big orange pussycat with bright green eyes. Just picturing Gia reading her books in it makes my heart glad. Then John remembered two tiny spool chairs he once found and he spent days sanding them and those were painted as well.

The hardest part was finding little 1950s pussycat decals to stick on the chairs, and I ended up ordering them online and then tried to find a local company to make them with a sticky back, which I did, but it took four days.

There is no one else I would do this for. And I wouldn't have been able to complete it without my friend Yvonne. That's what I love about living in a small place. You always know who to call.

We gave them their Advent calendars when we went up in November so they could use them this year, and every day on Zoom I see the big tree on the calendar fill up with decorations.

So far, Gia's favourite is a big white button. I like that one too.

TRAVELLING

"I"

JOHN AND I TRAVELLED WITH MY COUSIN AND HER HUSBAND TO OTTAWA ON THE weekend to attend my niece's wedding reception, which was held for all the deadbeats who were too cheap to go to her actual nuptials in Mexico last March.

It brought back memories of when the four of us hopped in a car and drove non-stop from Sydney to Montreal to attend my sister's wedding. On that occasion, Barb and I each packed a pair of underwear and a dress. We cranked the radio and sang at the top of our lungs while downing bags of greasy french fries and were most concerned whether we had enough beer and cigarettes for the trip.

Travelling in your sixties is a vastly different experience, but unfortunately you forget that until you go. In our minds, we were still those crazy kids who whooped it up across Canada.

First of all, we had more pills with us than clothes. We could have opened our own pharmacy at the airport. I have to carry a CPAP machine, which is mortifying. Recently the government made it mandatory to open the case in the security line to make sure I'm not hiding a concealed weapon. Now everyone knows that I look like a jet pilot when I sleep. CPAP stands for Chronically Pathetic Ashamed Person.

Trying to take a bag small enough to fit in the bin above your head on the aircraft means making major decisions. Do you take the hairdryer, curling iron, and flat iron, or just turn up at the party with ugly hair? In the seventies, we let our long locks fly free. Now we need to be plugged into a power socket to resemble the best version of ourselves.

Once upon a time, partying outside was preferable, weather be damned, but we've turned into our grandparents, and I'm sorry, but men complain the most.

"It's raining."

"Yes."

"We have to sit outside under a tent."

"Yes."

"It's cold."

"Yes."

"My hands are curling up."

"Go inside."

"This chair is hard. I can't feel my back."

"I need a drink."

Despite a few glitches, it was a marvellous time with family. A time to create memories. And now I have a great one of my intrepid cousin Barbara going up to our gate at Pearson Airport (clearly marked SYDNEY), and demanding to know who changed the gates without telling us and how were we going to get across the airport in five minutes because now we were going to miss our flight! But even better, her husband and I followed behind her like little ducklings, bubbling with indignation, as she roared off to catch the plane to Halifax.

Hubby had to screech at her from the top of an escalator that we weren't going to Halifax. We were going to Sydney.

We've lost a few trillion brain cells since that first car trip.

HANDS DOWN

"**/**,"

MY HAND IS OUT OF COMMISSION.

It's a total sob story as to how it happened, but basically my sick cat bit me. And because he's sick I can't be mad at him, but I am. My mistake was cleaning his face with a soft facecloth, as if he was a baby. He decided this was the last straw. He bit me so hard I couldn't get him off me. He hung on for at least fifteen seconds as I tried to open his mouth without hurting him. When I saw the two deep puncture wounds, I knew I was in trouble.

And I started to cry because it hurt very badly. But what do you do when it's a sick pet who obviously didn't mean it? Sort of. Who can you blame?

Hubby.

He is trying to fix Neo. All the fixing in the world is not going to make Neo better. We are at war over this cat. I love him dearly but I don't want him to suffer. Like I'm suffering.

"This is your fault!" I shout when hubby walks in the door.

"What did I do?"

Tearfully, I tell him my tale of woe. He tells me that Neo is very sorry and Neo is actually crying, he feels so bad.

For a second, I believe him, and then come to my senses. "No, he's not! You're just saying that."

"I swear! He just told me he feels terrible about the situation."

Why does this make me feel better?

Still, I quiver with indignation. "I am not giving him any more pills,

51

liquid, ointment, or food, because it involves his mouth, and I'm not going near that sucker for the foreseeable future!"

"Don't worry," hubby soothes. "I'll take care of everything."

I mope to bed, and when I wake up, there's my hand, bright red and swollen; so much so that I can't touch it, and if I accidentally brush up against something, I yell. For hubby.

"Look at this! This is your fault!"

Even he looks concerned. "Go to the doctor. That looks miserable."

So, I take my miserable self to the doctor. He takes one look at it and asks when I last had a tetanus shot.

"I can't remember."

"Roll up your sleeve."

Then he puts me on antibiotics and gives me an antibiotic cream to slather on it, and he wants to see me in three days. "If you see a red streak go up your arm, get to the hospital. We don't want blood poisoning or cellulitis."

Cellulitis? Isn't that dangerous? Is that when a cat scratches you and suddenly your hand falls off? As well as your nose? You see that all the time in articles on the internet. I'll try not to think about it.

So off I go and suddenly my life changes. When your right hand is out of commission and you can't touch anything without it being extremely painful, you find you don't want to do anything. Certainly not the dishes. Or cutting up vegetables. Or sweeping. Or dusting.

Wait, I don't do that anyway. Still, if I did, I can't do it now. I also scream when I put on my jacket to go for a walk, and have to soap up in the shower with my left hand. It feels odd and not very effective.

There's no way I could go to a book signing at the moment, since I can't hold anything, which is seriously curtailing my crossword puzzle addiction. Hubby happens to walk by as I am attempting it.

"This is your fault! I can't feel the pen! My fist is the size of a baseball glove and it's useless!"

"Neo is very, very sorry. He's still crying about it."

"And so he should. It's upsetting and unfair. Where do you keep your chocolate bars?"

"You don't want to do that, Lesley. You'll hate yourself in the morning."

"That's fine! Because I hate you and Neo right now."

This morning my puncture wounds are seeping. (Hope you're not reading this over breakfast.) I decide to go for a walk, gingerly putting on my jacket and even patting Neo on the head before I go out. He does seem sorry.

And then while I'm pouting down the laneway, a rabbit bounds out of the woods, heads straight for me, and hops up to my shoe.

This is the third time this has happened. It's my mother, trying to make me feel better. Once more, I can't believe it, but I think she wants to give me a hug. You always need your mom's hug when you feel rotten.

The rabbit hears all about it.

"It's hubby's fault."

She agrees with me.

THE BOOK SIGNING

"I"

BEING A WRITER REQUIRES ME TO BE ALONE A LOT OF THE TIME. I'M NOT ONE OF THESE people who can whip up a column or screenplay while typing at a small table at Starbucks. Young writers don't have a problem with this type of environment, but old-timers like me need to be in a tomb, where no noise or interruption can pierce my flighty thoughts. Even taking a sip of tea can cause me to forget what chapter I'm on or the name of the lead character.

Because writers like to be alone, it's often a daunting experience to have to interact with the public while promoting a new book. Publishers send you out into the world with a gentle shove and expect you to hold up your end of the bargain. Go sit on a stool outside a bookstore for two hours and sell as many copies as you can. Sounds easy.

It's not.

First of all, the chairs are always uncomfortable when you have a big arse, and you are acutely aware that people can see you spilling over the sides. Then you have to deal with the fact that shoppers are horrified to see you sitting there, because that means they can't just breeze into the bookstore. They must look for an alternate route so they can pretend not to notice you. The last thing they want is to make eye contact. And it's not because people are mean. They just don't want to hurt your feelings, because they really don't want your stupid book. They want to pick out the book they want. I get it. I do the same thing.

And the really funny thing is, everyone avoids you differently. There are ones who practically look at the ceiling, so they can be sure they are not looking at you, the desk, the books, the chair, my purse, or my pen. They usually bump into the end of aisles. Then there are the people who do look at me but give me a real stare, as if daring me to get off the chair and chase them to the back of the store.

After that you get the softies, who give you apologetic grimaces and shrug their way past you. You're left to guess if it's because they have no money or they just don't read on principle. Some people do manage to totally ignore you, as if you literally don't exist. It's like being shunned in the cafeteria in Grade Seven.

Then there are the people who are sort of interested, but they don't want to seem interested, so they circle the table several times, pretending to look at other books, while sneaking peeks at your covers.

Fortunately for me, I've developed a strategy that works almost 100 percent of the time: smiling. Even at the ones trying hard to distance themselves. Being pleasant and saying kind things out loud works, and because of my motherly persona, I can get away with telling a young woman that she's a beautiful girl. Now if an old male writer said that, he'd be slapped, so I have an advantage.

When you compliment someone and they aren't expecting it, they give you a real smile. It costs nothing to tell someone their baby is gorgeous. While I was in Montreal at Indigo, my table was set up opposite an escalator and moving up and down in front of me was an amazing array of people, all of them unique and I told them so. "You two could be models!" I shouted at two teenage girls. They giggled and waved, and then waved again when they had to go past me twenty minutes later.

They didn't buy a book, but that's okay. Being kind is more important.

ROCKY

"**!**"

IT'S NERVE-WRACKING TO KNOW I HAVE A ZOOM BOOK CLUB GET-TOGETHER TOMORROW with actual people staring at me over the computer. This is causing me major anxiety, as I haven't been to a hairdresser since late February, almost three months ago. Not only that, I was hit in the face by a flying squirrel yesterday. I'm a vision.

My assailant wasn't an actual flying squirrel but a little jerk ground squirrel who decided to be an asshole. And I do not say that lightly. You all know how much I love animals.

I was minding my own business carrying a bucket of veggie peels out to the compost bin in my usual shapeless nightgown, and it was sprinkling out, so my head was down as I walked around the corner of the house.

WOOOMMMPPPP.

Literally, I had no idea what hit me. My neck actually rocked back, and in that split second I realized that the black object flying through the air out of the corner of my eye was actually a squirrel who was scaling the house trying to get to the bird feeder in the upstairs window. The only reason I knew it was a squirrel is because after he hit my face, he used my cheekbone like a trampoline to propel himself eight feet through the air and scurry under the shed.

I stood there holding my eye, the vegetable peels still safely in my grasp.

"You complete moron!"

Into the house I go, yelling for hubby. "Is my eye bleeding?"

"What?!"

"My eye, my cheek! Is anything bleeding?"

"Why would it be bleeding? You only went out two seconds ago."

"Because that jeezly squirrel you feed all winter decided to do a triple flip on my face!"

He looked at me. "How does a squirrel hit you in the face?"

"Perfectly! He got a ten out of ten from the judges."

"Are you okay?"

"Of course not! This is 2020, isn't it?!! Why wouldn't I be hit in the face by Rocky the flying squirrel? Bullwinkle is probably out there too."

THE BLACK THUMB
OF DEATH

"I"

MY MOTHER WAS A WONDERFUL GARDENER. SO IS MY SISTER. JUST CALL ME THE anti-Christ of plants.

The cruel irony is that I love nature, flowers and vegetables, and growing, living things. Nothing gives me more pleasure than seeing a beautiful garden, be it someone's backyard, a field of buttercups and daisies, or a formal setting. Going to the British Isles cemented my love for English country gardens. I listen with envy to gardening programs on the radio and watch snippets of garden segments on talk shows and it all looks so incredibly easy when an expert does it.

But that is not my experience when I attempt it, because I have no patience when it comes to reading the information card stuck in flower pots, which is ridiculous since there are only about ten words on it, so I end up sticking things in exactly the wrong place every time and forgetting the names of the plants. My specialty is putting flowers that are two feet tall in amongst ground cover, not knowing the difference.

Now that wild lupins are overtaking my small rock garden, I don't have to weed or worry about the plants I put in there thirty years ago. All I remember about planting window boxes are the blasted blackflies and bug jackets and bug spray. I loathe having black earth under my fingernails, and hauling around mulch and manure is not high on my bucket list.

It's also a chore to water everything. We have flowers down at our cottage that we have to worry about even if we aren't there, so I'm forever feeling guilty if I don't drive down the road to top them up. Last year I put way too much earth in the cottage window boxes, and since the boxes are at a slant, all the water I poured in would just cascade right out, taking a lot of dirt with it every time and soaking me in the process.

Hubby asked me why I always get so jumpy when I'm in a garden centre. The real reason is I don't know what to buy. There is too much to choose from and I'm constantly worried I'll get the wrong thing. The whole process makes me panic, which is ridiculous. It's supposed to be relaxing.

I've killed every plant anyone has ever given me. But actually, I don't think I'm killing them. They are killing themselves because they know what's coming. "Oh crikey...it's Lesley Crewe's house. Abandon your post!"

My poinsettias look like the Grinch tiptoed into my living room when I wasn't looking. My attempts at drying hydrangeas usually go awry, and they end up looking like I've popped them in the toaster, shrivelling them to a minuscule size.

Plants are alive, so I know that they know when you're afraid of them. My sister loves everything about gardens and her plants sing in the back seat of the car when she drives them home.

Mine are choking back tears.

We bought a lot of flowers at the Masstown Market and I've put hubby in charge of them, so maybe this year they'll have a chance, but I did spy pots filled with different types of lettuce, kale, beets, and parsley. And I do love salad, so voila! Maybe I can keep this salad pot going.

It's only been five days and already it looks droopy. I'm watering, misting, doing my best to keep the cats from noshing on it, and it still looks rather unhappy. Maybe I'm cutting off too much at a time. I'd really like to keep this thing going if possible.

Last year my neighbour asked me if I'd "babysit" her basil plant. I warned her that I was the kiss of death, but she went on her vacation anyway. I was seriously spooked that I was going to kill it before she left the Causeway, so I talked to it, stroked it, watered it, and moved it around so the sun could get at it.

It was still alive when she came back, but I'm sure I saw that ungrateful basil hug her with relief before I left the kitchen.

P.S. The lettuce pots croaked.

EXCITEMENT

"/"

LET'S COUNT THE AMAZING THINGS THAT HAPPENED THIS WEEK IN THE LAND OF "STAY the Blazes Home."

Another squirrel report!

A squirrel ran away with a corn cob that was too big for him. He balanced both ends across the lawn as if he was a Flying Wallendas acrobat making his way across a high wire. It was so heavy, most of the time his little back feet were in the air. This was more amusing than if I'd paid a ticket to see a one-man show on Broadway. It's amazing what counts as entertainment these days.

Finally saw the most important person in my life, my hairdresser, Sheila. It's stunning that we can still talk a blue streak with masks on. She's helping me go grey, by putting in a few streaks. (Not blue.) She might as well since my scalp looks like a skunk is draped on it. For some reason she gave me purple shampoo. It's like putting ink on your head.

Hubby had a birthday yesterday. We had a family Zoom party and everyone sang "Happy Birthday" off-key, and not at the same time. No matter how hard I tried, I couldn't get the lighter working for the candles. And the cake split into three pieces at the top, which has never happened to me before in an entire lifetime of baking cakes, but this is 2020. When I gave him his gifts, the first thing out of his mouth was, "Shit. Now I have to get you something."

We always say we are not buying each other anything for our birthdays, and I went back on my word. But technically I didn't buy anything, because I got the wrong size, so now I have to take the three stupid shirts back to the lousy store. The first store I've actually been in for three months! I risked life and limb for those darn shirts.

We woke up this morning to go for our walk and a terrible smoky haze greeted us as we opened the door. A policeman happened to drive by and told us there was a fire at the local dump. We ran back inside to close the windows.

How are you supposed to stay the blazes home when the blaze is coming straight for your house? You watch. A UFO is going to land on the lawn tomorrow, but I'm okay with that. I just had my hair done.

STYLISH

"**!**"

THE OTHER DAY I RAN INTO A LOVELY GAL AT THE MALL, WHERE I WAS PICKING UP A couple of things after my exercise class, so I was in my usual uniform of black gym pants, grey exercise top, black puffy jacket, and old boots. Even my purse was a black nylon rag-bag affair. In other words, I looked about as exciting as a placemat.

When I was rushing past the food court I heard my name, and Arlene, who also goes to the exercise class, stopped me to say hello. While we exchanged pleasantries, I was distracted by how lovely she looked. This wasn't a Saturday night. How come she looked so put together only a few scant hours after doing jumping jacks?

She had make-up on, and her hair was just so, and she was wearing lots of shiny jewelry and bright clothes, with a colourful scarf around her neck. She looked like I might look if I was being given an OBE by the Queen, but it was a Thursday afternoon at the Mayflower Mall.

Finally, I blurted, "You look fantastic. Do you always dress up when you go shopping?"

She laughed. "I take after my mother. She always made an effort."

And that got me thinking about my mother. She always looked like a million bucks, in a classic, elegant way, even when she was on the beach. She was a beautiful woman with a slender figure, so clothes always looked great on her. And no one wore shoes like Mom. She had a closet full of fine Italian leather shoes. The sort I couldn't get past my big toe.

While spectacularly jealous of her ability to look like royalty, I was always so proud to introduce her as my mother. It was the way she held herself. Always straight and tall, her long legs striding forward with purpose. She was definitely a lovely hare, who ended up with a tortoise for a daughter.

I was clunky and chunky, with a hippie sensibility. Happiest in a wool poncho and Birkenstocks. My mother often despaired over my lack of fashion, but she didn't harp on it. Except for the moment when hubby proposed to me. I ran into the kitchen to tell her and the first thing she said was, "Oh, Lesley! Look at your shirt!"

The fact that he asked me to marry him while I was wearing an old, oversized red flannel shirt let me know that he didn't care what I looked like. And neither did I, obviously.

Mom would be happy to know that while her stylish genes may have skipped a generation, they have been passed down to her granddaughter. My daughter puts me to shame with her stylin' self. She's another one I'm spectacularly jealous of. Her ability to look freakin' fabulous amazes me, but then she'll turn around and be a slobby tortoise too, which is a comfort, because this is the state I'm familiar with.

All that said, as I left the nicely put together woman at the mall, she did give me pause. The fact that I noticed she looked lovely means that most of us *do* pay attention to how other people dress, and if that's so, what kind of an impression am I leaving as I schlep through the mall in my horrifically drab and dreary outfit?

It obviously says I don't care about myself, and that's not true. Taking a few moments to spruce myself up would remind me that I'm important and need to feel good about myself too.

So, the next time you see me in my blah clothes, I do hope I'm wearing a pair of bright red dangly tassel earrings and neon blue eye shadow.

I said I'd spruce myself up, but I never said anything about taste.

MY LITTLE APPLE

"**!**"

WHEN I LOVE SOMETHING, IT BECOMES MINE.
My latest acquisition is a tiny brown shrivelled apple on a small apple tree at the end of our laneway. It's near the old Spencer homestead. The original farmhouse was built around 1800, but it burned down. All that was left was the porch, and this farmhouse was built around a hundred and fifty years ago. It's a lovely old place.

Surrounding the farmhouse are the remains of an apple orchard. A lot of the trees you can't even see anymore because other evergreens and alders have taken over, but there is one tree that is close to the road and our neighbour tells me the apple variety is called a Transparent. The deer love to eat these treats, and you often see apples on the ground with a bite mark taken out of them.

Because I walk every day, I see the life cycle of these apple trees; I see when the pink-and-white buds start to peek out in the spring, and when the apple blossoms bloom with their glorious scent. I've often just plunked my face in the middle of them and inhaled deeply, but that can be dangerous. Other insects like plunking their faces into these flowers too.

Gradually the apples start to fall, and I noticed this one little apple at the end of the summer only because it was in such a peculiar spot on the tree. It had grown on a very small awkward little branch near the bottom of the trunk. It wasn't hanging off the branch; it looked like it was hugging the branch.

As the fall went on, I would go by and wave to this little apple, who eventually turned a lovely shade of russet. All her brother and sisters had bid farewell to their mama and were scattered around her feet. But my little apple was still hugging her. A mama's girl for sure.

Then I began to worry about winter. Surely this time of year would be dangerous. Before we left to spend Christmas in Halifax, I said goodbye to my little apple and wished her well. To my relief, she was here to greet me when I got back.

Our first snowstorm blew in the first week of January and the snow was heavy and wet and the wind was wild. All our trees and bushes were drooping under the weight of the snow, so I spent a lot of time clearing them with a broom. Once the plow went down our laneway overnight, I got up first thing and walked down the road to see if my little apple was still on the tree after all that mayhem. The wind is always worse down there because the farmhouse is near the water and the gales sweep over the sandbar and whistle their way along the fields.

She was still hugging her mama! I couldn't believe it. It made me so happy.

She's just a little apple, but she's become a symbol for me to hang on during the hard times and be grateful for every sunrise and sunset. If the day ever comes when she finally lets go, I'm taking her home with me.

Her name is Betty.

SMALL CHANGES

"I"

OKAY, IT'S JANUARY. ACTUALLY, JANUARY IS ALMOST OVER, BUT IT STILL COUNTS. The month when resolutions are made, but this is a daunting word and one I have a terrible track record with, so I'm avoiding this expression in 2019.

I've realized I have a few old habits that need to be addressed. Ruts, if you will. Nothing earth-shattering, but irritating, and now that I've noticed, I'm going to practice putting my stuck horse and cart back on the road.

There's the fact that I have forty candles in this house and I never light them.

This is a sad state of affairs. Why do I buy them if I'm not going to enjoy them? Because the minute I light them, I start thinking I'll forget to blow them out and the house will catch on fire. What a sad commentary on my inner dialogue. So, I've resolved to light candles, sit and stare at them, and then blow them out when I leave the room. Which doesn't sound pleasant, but what other choice do I have? I'm afraid they're up to no good when my back is turned. It's better than never lighting them at all, isn't it?

Come to think of it, the solution to my dilemma is sitting and relaxing.

My problem continues with hand and dishtowels. I have holiday towels and a few very nice dishtowels, but I never use them, which is ridiculous. Think of the joy I'd get wiping dishes with my Eiffel Tower towel (say that three times quickly), which I bought when I was in Paris. It would be nice to remind myself that I was actually there.

This year I'm going to dry my hands all over Santa Claus's face in my bathroom.

While I've written in a diary every day for many years, there are now so many that I've actually thrown some away because I have no room for them. Which makes me feel slightly guilty, but then I remember that my life is a bore and no one will miss them, least of all me. It would be different if I wrote about interesting things, like the sound of rain beating against the roof, or the smell of homemade bread when you come in from the cold.

But it's mostly, "Saturday, November 10, 2018. Rain all day. Made a pot roast. Watched movie. Blew my nose. Grumpy."

Blew my nose? Future generations will glean nothing from this. How can I make my diaries more interesting? But then I remember that sometimes I write all day, so by the time evening comes, I have nothing worthwhile to impart.

On my bureau is a cloth box my daughter made for me at art school, and I use it as a jewelry box. However, I never open it. There's also a small ornamental jewelry box my daughter-in-law brought me from Korea, which I never open either. These gifts of love are essentially a graveyard of necklaces, rings, and earrings. A jumbled pile, forgotten and forlorn.

Why? Jewelry makes me happy. How come I'm not wearing any?

Because the instant I put on a necklace, it turns a moldy green around my neck. With earrings, my earlobes become red, itchy, lumpy patches of flesh within mere minutes. If I jam on a ring, the only thing I achieve is a black mark around my finger. When your body hates jewelry, what are you supposed to do?

This sorry mess is getting to me. I'm going to get rid of the jewelry and use the boxes for other treasures, like letters, drawings, shells, and feathers.

My mother's costume jewelry is another matter. If I were crafty, I'd make a shadow box for some of her pieces and hang it on the wall, where I could see her every day. She's sick of being stuck in a drawer. But I'm not crafty, am I?

Looks like I have a lot of small things to achieve this year. And maybe that's the answer.

SHAME ON YOU

"**/**"

WHEN YOU LIVE IN THE COUNTRY AND YOUR GARBAGE BOX IS LARGE AND AWAY FROM prying eyes, there are despicable people who purposely drive up and dump their trash in that box. And if it doesn't all fit, they leave the rest of their mess strewn around it willy-nilly. Then they drive off.

This was the scene that greeted hubby this week. We have a substantial box next to the highway that the neighbours on our laneway share. It's always clean and we follow the rules. But because we can't see it from our living-room window, it is fair game for people who can't be bothered to drive to the dump.

Poor John was greeted with a soggy pile of plaster, wet cardboard, and other renovation material from a construction site, dropped on the ground and left without a thought for those of us who live here.

Needless to say, the air was blue while John surveyed the damage and stomped back to the house to gather expensive garbage bags, a shovel, and a rake. He spent three hours cleaning it up, and there was still more to be gathered, so he went back to the house and got an old steel garbage can from the backyard, dragged it up the road, and filled it with yet more plaster.

This is a lot of work for a man who is recovering his health. It makes me livid even thinking about it. (And before you ask why I wasn't up there with him; I was conveniently in Halifax living it up with our kids.)

Thinking the episode was over, he eventually went back to the house. The next day he awoke, fed the crows, and went for his walk with his cup of tea. He couldn't believe his eyes. There was the miserable plaster on the ground again. Someone had dumped the contents out and stolen the garbage can!

What is wrong with people? By all means, take stuff that's left out for the annual curbside giveaway, but would you take something that was obviously filled with trash, tip it over, and leave the mess on the ground?

It's like the time I put a wind chime in one of the birch trees over my mother's grave. She was with me when I bought it, and it was the prettiest little thing, with the sun and moon engraved in it. The next time I went to tend to her flowers, it was gone. Since I had had to get up on a ladder to put it on the branch, it couldn't have been easy to get it down. My anger knew no bounds.

So, I fired off a letter to the editor of our local paper and wrote that I put the sweet wind chime in that pretty tree to keep my wonderful mother company as she lay under the stars at night.

Two days later, I returned to the cemetery and there it was, hanging in the same spot with fishing line. Back to my desk to write another letter to the editor, thanking the person who put it there, saying I hoped they felt better, because I sure did.

Not to mention the time I bought a beautiful cedar Christmas wreath covered with pine cones and holly berries to put on our baby son's grave. It was stolen a day later.

People who litter and steal are thoughtless. You'd have to be thoughtless, because if you thought about what you were doing, wouldn't you be ashamed of yourself? I'll never understand the mind that only wants what it wants, regardless of how it makes others feel.

How do you handle bad apples? How do you get through to them?

I'm tempted to set up cameras everywhere to catch them in the act, but does that make me as creepy as them?

SENSITIVE SOULS

"**/**"

THERE WAS NO CHOICE FOR ME TO BE ANYTHING OTHER THAN A SENSITIVE SOUL. I grew up with a mother who never knew that the three blind mice had their tails chopped off. Her mother excluded that bit of information, knowing it would scar her mentally. I am nothing if not my mother in this regard.

My first reaction to anything is to run away. Ask my kids. They'd come in the door bleeding, and I'd scream and head in the other direction. I wouldn't come out of the closet until hubby yelled that the kids would live. Heaven knows what kind of damage I've done to their psyche, knowing their mother will only save them when the coast is clear.

All my life I've been ashamed of this behaviour. That is until recently, when a psychiatrist told me that I was only protecting myself. Well, that makes sense, doesn't it? But it still feels like a bit of a cop-out. Mothers are supposed to be warriors, especially if their children are involved.

I'd like to think that if my children were in real danger, I'd morph into a grizzly bear and shred the offending party into tiny pieces, instead of becoming a human hermit crab. Hopefully we'll never have to find out.

But it's not only other people I wimp out on. I don't stick up for myself either, and I was the big marshmallow in the schoolyard who absorbed the mean words thrown my way instead of lashing out with a saucy retort. That's why I love writing books. My heroines always get to say what I won't. Being a badass in fiction helps if you're a jellyfish in real life.

The timid in this world are unduly discriminated against. It's almost the last bastion of prejudice, along with being fat. We're still allowed to make fun of fat people, and if you're the type whose knees knock together, well, you're just next to useless.

Why is being gentle or meek or soft or weepy frowned upon? Surely in this dog-eat-dog world, where everyone criticizes every move you make, it would be a relief to run into a gooey person who just loves your scarf, or your dog, or your lip gloss, or your smile.

Now that I'm in my sixties, I still don't always say what I'd *really* like, but what I am doing is expressing myself out loud. So often, I'll be in a grocery lineup or walking through a big-box store or just coming out of a Tim Horton's, and I'll see something and straightaway say what I'm thinking.

With astonishing results.

"You girls look like you should be in a magazine...just gorgeous," I say to two fashionable girls smoking cigarettes in a parking lot. Obviously, I want to say *stop smoking*, but they're young and foolish, as was I, once upon a time. But their faces light up. No longer are they sort-of-surly-looking tough girls. One of them says, "Hey, you just made my day. Thank you!"

Which reminds me of the time I told a grocery clerk that she had the most beautiful complexion I'd ever seen.

"Complexion?" she said, unsure what I meant.

"Your skin is glowing. How perfect!"

She was still smiling when I left.

There have been times in my life where I wished I was the cool one, or the sassy and sophisticated one, but after all this time, I realize that is not my destiny. I'm perfectly happy being nice. Being nice is underrated. When I sit at a table outside a bookstore, I make it my mission to smile at everyone going by, even if they look right past me. Sometime people even frown at me, wondering if I'm as high as a kite.

All I know is that if I'm ever a grandmother, my grandchildren will be under the illusion that blind mice have tails, ding-dong bell, pussy isn't in the well, and ladybird, ladybird's house is not on fire and her children aren't all gone.

ROAD TRIP

"**/**"

I T'S CLEAR FROM THIS LAST TWO-DAY ROAD TRIP HUBBY AND I EMBARKED ON THAT you can't take me anywhere and I have no idea what's going on most of the time. And it really bothers me when hubby points this out.

It was me who got the directions from various sources, like emails, Google Maps, my phone, the horse's mouth, etc. Every one of these sources turned out to be wrong. That's not true. They weren't wrong, I just wrote out the wrong directions, read the wrong email, talked to the wrong horse, and so we ended up going around in circles for a time, until hubby sorted it out.

"How are you going to manage without me?"

Quite nicely, I'm sure, since I won't have him around telling me how I can't manage without him.

But I started to think he was right after I was half an hour late for a book reading yesterday. Thirty whole minutes. Mortified, I looked back in my correspondence, and sure enough, it said to arrive at six thirty. Hubby had asked me what time I had to be there.

"Seven o'clock."

"Are you sure?"

"Yes!"

Then, every single time I left the hotel room, I started down the hallway the wrong way. Fine, do it once, that's understandable. Maybe even twice. But I did it at least twenty times, completely convinced the elevator was on the exact opposite end of the corridor.

And can I just say that Truro is not the town to be in if you have no sense of direction? There doesn't seem to be a clear way in or out. It's like a giant maze, just waiting for people like me to wander in and never leave.

We did manage to find our way to Masstown Market, after traffic tie-ups that seemed to be going on exactly at the entrance and exit of the place. But my goodness, it was worth the wait. And this is where the worst incident happened. We decided to have lunch there. All of it looked so good, but we dithered and poked around like my grandmother used to do.

"What do you want?"

"I don't know. You?"

"Not sure."

"I'll have seafood chowder."

"So will I."

Then I went off to look for something to drink. Hubby got milk and I rooted through the water and juices. Since I'm now reading labels for calorie counts (and don't say it, I knew the seafood chowder was at least 100 points), I recoiled at the 200-calorie lemonade and thought, nuts to this, so I picked up a coconut-and-pineapple water at 25 calories.

As I paid for it, it occurred to me that pineapple and coconut didn't have a whole lot in common with seafood, but I'd make do. There were now ten people behind me at the cash register.

We settled ourselves in a booth, and I opened my water. I took a swig, waiting for a burst of tropical loveliness. Nothing. I tasted it again.

"Boy, this stuff sure doesn't taste like pineapple or coconut."

Hubby didn't care. He was eating his chowder. I took another drag.

"This has got to be the mildest solution I've ever had. It actually tastes like water. What do you think?" I pass it to him.

"I'm not drinking that."

"Try it for me? Am I nuts?"

"Yes. And I'm still not trying it."

So, I started on my chowder, which was delicious. After drinking almost three quarters of the bottle, I noticed the cap. It looked funny and I picked it up. It read "Pull and Press."

There was a whole capful of coconut-and-pineapple flavouring inside this cap, and if I just pulled the label off and pressed down, the crystals would fall in the bottle and flavour it. How was I supposed to know? I told hubby and he grunted. After I pulled and pressed, the entire contents spilt out before I could measure a little, so now I had a Jell-O shot in the bottle. Like a mad woman I took a sip anyway, only to have Hawaiian chemicals lodge in the back of my throat.

The moral is, I can't leave Homeville.

RECIPES

"I"

IN MY PANIC TO FIGURE OUT WHAT KIND OF UNIQUE GIFT I COULD GIVE HUBBY FOR Christmas, I pounced on something he said in passing one day. About how he loved his mother's cookies and hadn't had them in years. They were chocolate drop cookies and raisin drop cookies. Apparently she was too busy to ever roll out dough, but she was a nurse, so that makes sense.

With glee, I decided that's what I'd make him for Christmas. Two whole cookie tins for his own private consumption. But that's when the hard part kicked in. Those recipes were somewhere, but I had no idea where exactly. It would require a reconnaissance mission of massive proportions, seeing as how I have recipes in books, boxes, files, bags, and folders shoved everywhere throughout the kitchen.

To gather them together took me two hours. Basically, I had to remove everything in the bottom of the kitchen hutch. It was amazing what was in there. Binoculars? A fondue set I'd forgotten I owned, boxes of school supplies, a ruler, lighters, an old glass microwave tray? How did that happen?

So, I set aside an evening when John was already enthralled with a British murder mystery on television and started to rifle through the boxes of recipes I've saved over forty years. Suddenly Mom and Grammie were sitting with me, as their handwriting leapt in front of my eyes. One of the recipes was written on a notepad from my dad's publishing company fifty years ago, so I kissed it.

But what I didn't realize was how often I've saved the same recipe over the course of my life. Chicken and dumplings seemed to be a perennial favourite. I've cut it out of a newspaper, a magazine, printed it off a computer, written it down on the back of a napkin and a birthday card. I've never made it.

There were eight lasagna recipes: meat, vegetarian, stovetop, casserole style, something called lasagna soup, which sounded awful, and all this time I've only ever used my mother's recipe because it's the best. Why am I keeping the others?

So now I was thinking to myself, since I have all ten thousand recipes in front of me, I should edit this lot, and save only the really, really good recipes that we actually use, or recipes I remember my grandmother making, or recipes that bring back lovely memories. Why am I saving someone else's million-dollar green tomato relish, if I haven't made it in four decades?

An hour into it, I finally ran across the raisin drop cookie recipe. Hurray! Then I realized I couldn't read all of it. The ink was faded in crucial spots. Drat and darn. It was in his mother's handwriting, and I remember the day she wrote it out for me. A cloud of gloom descended, until I reached into the box again and there was the recipe written out in my handwriting. Phew. I paper-clipped the two together. There's no way I'd throw out the faded one.

At the end of hour two, I was despairing. There weren't many recipes to go, and those chocolate drop cookies hadn't appeared yet, but I was sure I had the recipe. The funny part is, they're really weird cookies. An acquired taste, for sure. They look like someone threw a spoonful of chocolate cake batter from a great height onto a cookie sheet, flat and completely unappetizing to look at. But John has great memories of them, so I had to find it.

And I did. The second-to-last sheet of paper in the big box. If I had started at the back of the box, I'd have saved myself an entire hour of searching. I literally jumped up from the table and yelled, "YES!" while waving my hands in the air.

"What are you yelling about?" hubby shouted from the bedroom.

"Nothing. Leave me alone. It has nothing to do with you. It's none of your business. Stay in the bedroom."

"What?!"

"It's Christmastime! Don't ask me any questions at Christmas. There are secrets floating about. You'll ruin everything!"

He muttered something, but stayed where he was. He knows me by now. Hurriedly, I took my two recipes and ran to my study and put them in a safe place before I went back and gathered up the mess I'd made.

But looking at those recipes was a walk down memory lane, and I'm determined to use them in a project for myself in the coming months: to gather them up, throw out the unnecessary ones, sort them into categories, write down the memories associated with them, and put them in a scrapbook for myself, that will one day go to my kids.

It turns out, family recipes are the best diaries in the world.

THE PRISONER

"!"

DAY 4,739 OF CAPTIVITY.

Nothing to report. No activity. No signs of life in COVID-19 land.

Mother's Day celebrated with no kids or granddaughter. I laid my head on the kitchen table and drooled on the placemat. Alarmed, hubby stole some daffodils he found in a ditch and pretended this was a great gift to cheer me up and I pretended I liked it.

This morning, I plucked all the stiff white hairs out of my eyebrows and realized too late that I had no eyebrows left. Then I went after my chin hairs. I wish I could say I had no chins left.

Undaunted, I took my bottle of Ativan pills and cut them in half with a pill-splitter. Do you know how small stupid Ativan pills are? And they aren't even round! That makes it a frustrating task, but it did use up three hours, so there's that.

What did I find but five heads of broccoli in the fridge, which clearly indicates I need to clean out that sucker more often? Googled broccoli recipes. A rabbit hole if ever there was one.

Someone please stop me from watching Olivia Pope on *Scandal*. I'm only on season five and I want Huck to come in here and kill me, but I have two more seasons to go.

Looking for something to do, I cleaned out the top left-hand drawer in the bathroom. Did you know we have fifty-six little containers of floss from the dentist? Apparently, we never use them. Only the big one from Walmart. That ends today.

My ceiling fans are covered with dust around the edges. My grandmother would be mortified. I wish she was here. I'd have her up on a chair, pronto.

There's a big hole in my favourite dumpy sweater. Right by the neck. It's unravelling.

Like me.

OLD AGE

"I"

CHECKING THE MAILBOX THE OTHER DAY ON MY WAY HOME FROM THE GROCERY STORE, I found an envelope addressed to me. It was obviously government issue, but it gave no hint to what was inside, so I was well and truly shocked when I opened it and there in my hand was an application for my Old Age Security Pension.

I'm now entitled to a pension. For old age. These two things would suggest that according to the Government of Canada, I'm not a teenager anymore. And yet, in my head, I'm only seventeen, so someone in Ottawa got it wrong.

Now I have a whole year to reconcile the fact that I will be sixty-five on my next birthday. Sixty-five was always my grandfather and his buddies. Old men who smoked and drank coffee while shooting the breeze on their front steps. Geezers who talked about hockey and fishing. Guys who wore their trouser belts up around their rib cage.

A sixty-five-year-old woman in my childish mind was a lovely grand-mother or great-aunt type who wore an apron over their flowered dress, compression stockings, sensible shoes, and a hairnet. They always had candy in their apron pockets and walked around with a dust cloth. Absolute salt-of-the-earth ladies, who could take splinters out with a needle and double-knot your shoelaces at the same time.

They seemed like a different species. Now here I am at their age, but on the inside I'm still the same silly, insecure, fretful bowl of jelly I've always been. So, did they feel like that too? Were they still unsure about life, even though they seemed as strong and as powerful as tree trunks back then?

It's a very odd sensation to reconcile the "you" on the inside with the you who rode your bike fearlessly down Montreal sidewalks and slow danced the night away in a sexy dress, with the you looking in the mirror with saggy eyelids and blotchy skin. How did that happen, and why didn't you notice the years falling away day after day?

My initial reaction to this application was dismay. But it very quickly turned to gratitude. This is just another rite of passage, and I've been lucky enough to live this long, and to get to see this day. Some of my dear friends would have loved this privilege, would've given anything to be sixty-five, or sixty, or fifty-five.

So, here I am, finally in on a big secret. You still feel like a kid on the inside when you go to the mailbox to pick up your pension cheque. Mind you, the kid is a bit tattered and beaten up and rough around the edges, but you're still in there.

And it's sort of reassuring that little kids think you're wise and have all the answers, just because you have grey hair and wrinkles. If only they knew the real story; but we'll keep that a secret, along with Santa Claus and the Easter Bunny.

My mom told me that she still felt like a young woman at the age of seventy-two, as they carted her off to fix her heart. She didn't make it through that surgery, and it makes me so sad to think that she still had lots of childish things to do. The age of seventy-two is not so old anymore, especially when you're about to turn sixty-five.

It all comes down to being incredibly grateful for every day you're given. Even the lousy ones, because then there's always time to try and fix them.

People say that what's great about getting older is you don't care what people think of you anymore. Well, I still struggle with that because I'm a big chicken. There's also the notion that you can say whatever you want at this age. But considering the times we live in, I'd be very reluctant to say anything, because internet trolls will eat you for breakfast.

My plan is to have a tiny party when I get my first pension cheque. Just me and hubby. Maybe he'll finally let me buy him a pair of slippers that cost more than fifteen bucks.

MY STUPID POT

"**/**"

WHEN I FINALLY GOT AROUND TO MUCKING OUT MY KITCHEN, IT TOOK ME THREE DAYS because I removed everything off the walls, from inside the cupboards, off the counter, and even took down the window blinds to soak in the bathtub. This was a serious mission, to the point that I removed every last can from the pantry and scoured the inside, even the top shelf that I can only access with a ladder. It's a good thing I did. There was a can of pears from 2003 that had been lurking like nuclear waste in the very back.

While I was in this manic state, I decided to biff the items that were no longer serving a purpose, the stuff I wouldn't dream of handing off to someone else at Goodwill. Two pots qualified, and an old electric frying pan that has been languishing underneath the sink, almost getting moldy. The only reason I hung on to it was because it was my mother's, but I can hear her voice in my head: "Don't blame me for the appalling state of that frying pan! It was pristine when I gave it to you."

That was always her favourite word. *Pristine.* Well, it's the exact opposite now. So, I made a little pile of the things no longer serving a purpose and hid them from hubby, because he has an obsessive need to make sure nothing is ever thrown out. I've actually gone to the garbage box under the cover of darkness to get rid of something. It's my version of a spy mission. My heart races in case I get caught. The pressure is unreal.

So now I have only one small pot and we really need two. There are bigger pots, but if I'm making hardboiled eggs and hubby wants to steam a few carrots and green beans for himself, we need two before he starts interrogating me on the disappearance of kitchen items.

The race was on to go to Walmart and stand in front of the shelves of pots. There was another couple, speaking German, doing the exact same thing. Too bad I don't understand German, because I think they were having an argument and I'm just naturally nosy, so I was distracted in my own search. I'm blaming this couple for what I ended up with. That and my cheapskate ways are the reasons I picked up a pot that I am now regretting, big time.

Care and use instructions should always be where you can see them before you buy a product. Once you rip off the plastic gunk covering up the item, it's too late to do anything about it. The small slip of paper saying wash with hot soapy water before using, I was prepared for, but this miserable pot came with an entire foolscap sheet of directions. It was tempting not to read it, but once again, my nosy nature did me in and I scanned every line.

Boy, am I sorry I did. This lousy pot needs more babysitting than a grandchild.

Naturally, the wash in hot soapy water using a soft cloth was there, as well as making sure to dry completely. But then, get this: "It's recommended to add a teaspoon of cooking oil prior to each use."

For real?! That's a couple of Weight Watchers points. No way am I doing that.

"Never heat an empty cooking utensil. Be sure there is oil, butter, liquid, or food before placing on range or burner."

Isn't that what we usually do? That's just silly. But then they really blew my socks off.

"It's not recommended to use on high heat."

It's a POT! A pot's only use is for you to put something in it and boil it as quickly as possible. I'm not going to stand by my stove gently coaxing this pot to do the one lousy thing it's supposed to do. Who has that kind of time?

"Cooking on excessive heat can cause warping. Never use utensils with sharp edges. Never use metal scouring pads. Only add salt to water after it comes to a boil, because salt grain deposit on the cookware bottom will ATTACK the metal as the heat melts it down. Never put cold water into a hot cooking utensil. If using a ceramic stovetop, LIFT the pan rather than sliding it across the glass plate. Higher cooking temperatures can cause the handle to get hot. Shine of the coating may become dull and discoloured due to the action of certain detergents. Handle may become loose with use."

Apparently, this pot is a non-stick sucker, which I never noticed because

I was too interested in the arguing duo.

Needless to say, I haven't even used this fragile flower of a pot and I hate it. My plan is to do everything I am not supposed to do, so that it will die an early death and stop bugging me. And then I'm going down to the bungalow and grab one of my grandmother's old battered pots that has been happily boiling water for eighty years without freaking out and moaning about its precious needs.

MOTHERS

"I"

BOY, THIS TOPIC IS A CAN OF WORMS, OR BEANS, OR CHICKEN SOUP. YOU KNOW mothers. They feed you regardless of what's going on. And that's the wonderful thing about mothers. Except when you are a vegan and they are trying to stuff a turkey dinner down your gullet.

Pick any topic. It doesn't have to be about food. Your mother always has something to say about clothes. Yours in particular.

"You are not going out wearing that."

"Over my dead body."

"But Great-Aunt Mildred made that knitted hat with ringlets for the baby! She has to wear it to the christening."

"Why not wear my wedding dress on your big day?"

They also have opinions on your house. It's too cold, it's too hot, it's too dirty.

"Why in God's name do you let that dog on the couch? It doesn't take a genius to figure out why your last couch is toast."

Mothers are the backseat drivers of your life, never mind the car. And they can drive you around the bend faster than anyone else, but have a disaster happen and we have mom on speed-dial.

"Stay right there, sweetheart. I'm coming to get you."

"Your boss is a big knob and I'm going to tell him so."

"Your boyfriend is an even bigger knob and if he steps one foot in this door, it's curtains for him!"

"Never mind, honey. You'll do better next time. Would you like some pie?"

Only when your mom is gone do you realize what a treasure she was. Who else in the world keeps your report card from Grade Two? Or puts your painting in a frame and hangs it on the wall? She knows your favourite meal, your favourite cookie, your best friend's nickname, how much you have in your bank account, and how to make you laugh.

Or cry.

Moms are good at that too. No one could make me cry harder than my mother, if I thought she was being mean to me. OR HOW SHE DIDN'T UNDERSTAND A SINGLE THING ABOUT ANYTHING IN THE ENTIRE UNIVERSE! AND I'M NEVER COMING OUT OF MY ROOM FOR THE REST OF MY LIFE!

Luckily, she was always there when I did slink out of my room.

The house always seems empty when your mom isn't home. It doesn't matter if there are ten other people in the house. If mom isn't around, it's not quite the same.

And now my mom isn't with me. I've been missing her for sixteen years. [Author's note: Make that twenty-one.] And I swear to God, it doesn't get any easier. I'm so spectacularly jealous when I see women my age with their mothers. Do they know how lucky they are? I can spot them in grocery stores or coffee shops. The ease with which they stay close, talk a little, or gaze out the window. I want to talk to my mom about what it feels like to become a grandmother for the first time, or what she would recommend for sore knees. Did she mind getting wrinkles and grey hair? Did she ever feel like hitting her retired husband over the head with a frying pan? These are life's mysteries that need to be shared, and I miss not sharing them.

And then there's the fact that she never read any of my novels. Or saw my movie. All the work she said I was capable of has finally come to fruition, but she's not here to share it with me. The accomplishment is not the same when your mother isn't here to give you a hug.

Luckily, my own children hug me instead, and so the story continues.

Happy Mother's Day.

MANI-PEDI

L OVE, LOVE, LOVE HAVING SOMEONE GIVE ME A MANICURE AND PEDICURE.
Hate, hate, hate trying to decide on a colour.

I almost don't go because I cannot abide trying to figure out which shade I should choose among the seventy-five coloured bottles on the wall. In my mind, it's like a trap. People will be able to define me by the colour I put on my hands and feet, which is utter nonsense. No one cares about my extremities, and yet it always seems of the utmost importance the moment I'm standing there trying to decide.

Finally, the poor nail gal comes over to hasten me along.

"Anything you like?"

"Umm. I'm not sure."

"Do you like dark colours or light colours?"

"Who's to say?"

She states the obvious. "You. It's up to you."

"Well, I don't mind darker colours on my toes, but I have a book tour and my nails need to be a bland colour."

"Why's that?"

"So, I can hopefully remember to wear gloves while washing dishes for the next two weeks and have the nails fade into a neutral colour that will last for another couple of weeks because I'm too cheap to come back here in three weeks and have this done again."

"You know you can get shellac nails that last a long time."

"Oh, dear, no. The last time I did that, I picked it all off and my real nails looked miserable when I managed to peel away the last of the shellac."

"Do you like blue?"

"No."

"Do you like green?"

"I don't want green toenails. People will think I'm moldy."

"What about yellow?"

"Good gravy. People will think I'm dying."

"Red?"

"Never."

"White?"

I shake my head. She's ready to bonk me on the head, but she's too sweet to admit it.

"What about this lovely navy blue, greyish colour? It's very popular."

Well, I like being popular, even if it is blue. "Okay."

She looks relieved. "How about this shade for your fingernails? It's like a beige colour. Your nails will disappear completely, if that's what you're going for."

Isn't that what everyone wants when they go for a manicure?

She looks at her watch. I panic. "Fine. That's great. Let's do it."

Just so she's clear, as she gets the foot bath ready, I let her know my preferences. "I like short nails."

"Fine."

"The shorter the better."

"Great."

"I don't like feeling my nails on the keyboard. It's a distraction."

"Is that so?"

"Sometimes I write for hours, so it can be annoying."

"Interesting."

This isn't interesting in the least, but she's too sweet to say so.

Glancing over at the lady in the next chair, I'm suddenly in love with the colour she's chosen for her feet. Something I wouldn't have picked in a million years, because I'm such a chicken.

"That's lovely," I say.

She splays her toes and we both look at them. "Aren't they?"

"What's the name of that colour?" I ask.

"Honky-Tonk Woman."

There ya go.

She feels she must return the favour. "Your toenail colour is nice as well. What's it called?"

"Melancholy Baby." Which explains a lot.

"And your fingernails?" she asks.

My nail gal speaks up for me. "This is called Flesh."

Oh, geez.

My neighbour tries not to look dismayed at my choice. She holds out her hand. "I thought I'd try Orange Popsicle on my first three fingers and Honey Greengrass Strawberry Swirl on the other two. You only live once."

Why am I not like this woman? Why do I stick with blah and comatose? These colours are not going to be on my nails for the rest of my life. In a matter of seconds, they will be chipped off, scrubbed off, stubbed off, or bitten off.

I'll gather up my courage for next time.

THE MOVIES

"**I**"

I LOVE GOING TO THE MOVIES.

The first movie I ever saw was *Mary Poppins*. The best part about it for me was the penguins. I'm not surprised, because I've always loved animals more than people. (Unless I know you. Then you're loved.)

Chitty Chitty Bang Bang was another doozy. When that car went flying in the air, it was exhilarating.

And what about the Beatles in *A Hard Day's Night*? They ran around a lot, although looking back, I don't think there was a plot. Who cares? It was the Beatles!

The best one was Franco Zeffirelli's *Romeo and Juliet* in 1968. I was thirteen, and to this day I don't think I've seen a finer bottom than Leonard Whiting's. And Olivia Hussey! We all wanted to look like her.

Fortunately, I've only had one bad experience in a movie theatre. My friend was on the end of the aisle and I was beside her. A man in our row kept moving closer to me throughout the movie, but since I only knew wonderful men like my father and Grampy, I wasn't alarmed until he reached over and rubbed his fingers on my leg. When I jumped two feet in the air, he scurried away, but I trembled until I got home.

Some of the best times I shared with my parents were movies we watched on television. *A Funny Thing Happened on the Way to the Forum* or *The Russians are Coming, The Russians Are Coming*, and *It's a Mad, Mad, Mad, Mad World*. I can still hear my dad laughing. If you've never seen these movies, do yourself a favour and look for them. The world needs laughter at the moment.

At this point in my life, going to the Sydney Cineplex is as exotic a date as hubby and I can muster. And we'd rather go in the afternoon, which makes us even more pathetic. We always sit in the same seats, in the middle of the very back row. I'm not sure how we got so dreary. Oh, I remember. Hubby decided it would ruin his life if someone sneezed on him. (In hindsight, smart fellow). And since a date requires you to sit with the actual person, I have to sit in the back row too. This means we head for the cinema an hour ahead of time, so John can save the seats. I don't care anymore, because I just walk over to Pennington's and browse until the movie starts. Doesn't matter if it's dark. I know where to find him.

I'm one of those odd people who love to go to movies alone. That way you're not fighting over the armrest or poking someone in the ribs to get them to shut up and stop asking questions. I feel an instant affinity with the lone male teenager sitting with his large popcorn, and I want to tell him it doesn't matter that he doesn't have a girlfriend right now. He'll have a wonderful life down the road.

And then came the day when I was asked to write a screenplay for my first novel. Six years later, *Relative Happiness* played on the big screen in Sydney for five weeks, along with Hollywood blockbusters. I was too busy thinking to actually watch it, remembering when I wrote that particular scene and what I could've done better. All the years of work passed through my mind.

It wasn't until I was in a balcony in a playhouse at the St. John's International Women's Film Festival that I looked down at the almost eight hundred people below me, laughing and sniffling in the dark, that it hit me. This was my movie.

How I wished my parents were with me.

LITTLE SANDWICHES

"I"

THERE ARE A LOT OF WONDERFUL THINGS IN THIS OLD WORLD, BUT AT THE TOP OF the list have to be little sandwiches.

These magnificent creatures come out in full force in the summer months, thanks to bridal showers, weddings, family reunions, picnics, bungalow get-togethers, and graduation parties. They are with us all year long because of birthday celebrations, book club meetings, and funeral feasts, but summer is a time when more often than not, someone comes through your door with a tray of fresh white-bread triangles stuffed with succulent fillings.

We all have our favourites, the ones we gravitate to and hopefully grab before they are all gone. Egg salad sandwiches sound boring, but they are the go-to choice when you're not sure what the grey pâté-looking option is on the table to your left. Elevating the egg sandwich to an even more potent level is a layer of Cheez Whiz, making it a triple-decker threat. Amazing!

But is there anything that makes your eyes light up more than a lobster roll or shrimp or crab number? These are gone in a flash, and the people who bring them are heroes in our eyes. Imagine paying for lobster to stuff in a sandwich? Remember to invite these people to everything.

The shower sandwich I remember most growing up was the asparagus roll. It took me a while to even try it because it seemed so grown up, but once I did, I never looked back. Another oldie but goodie I happened upon recently is the cream-cheese-and-cherry sandwich. Cherries don't sound like sandwich material, but you try it. It's out of this world.

Ham and cheese are always a good choice, but to be really fancy, try ham and Brie. Flaked ham with little bits of pickle relish and mayonnaise just screams a good time. Tuna and salmon are popular, but the tuna needs to be solid white albacore to really make an impression, and not the brown cat-food-looking variety that you can smell from thirty paces. Salmon should be red if possible, and ideally, smoked!

Good old chicken salad sandwiches always disappear the second they are dropped on the table, but did you know that a vegetable sandwich is the most popular of all? The ordinary cucumber sandwich is the lord of the manor, followed by watercress. If it's good enough for the royals, it's okay by us.

Bridge clubs the world over know the delights of the pimiento-cheese-with-mayo-and-pecan number. I can still see this recipe in my mother's Betty Crocker cookbook. It was served with tomato aspic and Bloody Marys with celery sticking out of the glass. Ah...the fifties and sixties were so civilized.

Men in particular love to see their wives come home with an assorted plate of funeral sandwiches (that's hubby's name for them). And who can blame them? Not many of their get-togethers call for these itty-bitty snacks, so they are delighted with this treat. Which is sort of strange, because if you cut their regular lunch sandwiches into four pieces, they'd probably mention it. Only their mothers did that, and they're not kids anymore. The difference is the crust. If it stays on, it just looks weird cut into four, but if you cut the crusts off, suddenly you're in Julia Child territory.

And women love little sandwiches, because you can eat seventeen of these suckers and still convince yourself you only had one sandwich at most. Dividing things into smaller things means you're not eating as much. Everyone knows that, even people who aren't good at math.

There's probably another aspect to why we love finger sandwiches so much. We're usually with people we know and love when we're eating them, or at least at a friendly get-together. There are always cups of tea involved, and paper napkins, and usually gifts and streamers and lemonade. It's the whole atmosphere that makes us feel cozy and comforted. Trays of sandwiches on a kitchen counter usually mean that something good is about to happen. Or that at least we're together, if it's something bad.

The one trick my grandmother taught me is to always place a damp paper towel on top of the mound of delectable little sandwiches before you wrap them in plastic wrap and put them in the fridge. That way they are always moist and cold when you put them out on the table, and the bread is as fresh as a daisy.

The only downside is you have to try not eat them all before your guests arrive.

LIFE IS A HIGHWAY

"**/**"

L IFE IS A HIGHWAY. WHO SANG THAT? I'M ONLY KIDDING. EVERY CANADIAN KNOWS TOM Cochrane sang it, and every Canadian knows it's an earworm of epic proportion. Do not get this tune stuck in your head, especially if you're driving down a highway all night long.

You can come across every type of human being on a highway. How a person drives is the first clue as to who they are as a person. And it seems to me that not many of us like the people we share the road with. Sometimes we don't even like the people we share the car with.

If you ask me, very slow drivers cause more accidents than very fast drivers. That's because very slow drivers make the rest of us become very fast drivers, in a bid to get rid of them. The only time I ever drive over the speed limit is when I'm behind a car that's pulling a tent trailer and they've been going forty kilometres an hour for the last thirty minutes. The moment a passing lane comes up, I stomp on the gas and become a Formula 1 driver, and now I'm basically a lunatic, trying to overtake seven cars before the passing lane runs out.

It's unnerving how quickly I change from being a sweet, motherly type to a raging warrior. And it's all that trailer guy's fault.

Driving isn't the only consideration when you're out on the highway. You have to negotiate the pee breaks and the food breaks and the coffee breaks. And no one ever agrees they need to do all three at the same time. This causes massive frustration, especially when there is a person in the car who is trying to gain weight, and a person in the car who is trying to lose weight.

"I'm going to get a coffee," hubby says.

"Is that all?"

"Yes."

"Okay, I'll have one too."

He comes back to the car with two coffees and a stupid bag.

"That better not have two doughnuts in it."

"It doesn't."

I look in it. It does.

"You jerk."

"I can't help it. I'm hungry."

"I've been hungry for sixty-two years!"

He eats the doughnuts while I stare out my window, giving him the cold shoulder.

But the worst situation on the highway is trying to figure out which way to go. Hubby has maps he's printed off, so why does he need me to check my phone? Then while I'm checking the phone, he yells, "What did that sign say?"

I look up. "What sign?"

"What does the phone say?"

I look down. "I can't get it to work. Oh wait, it says we still have sixteen thousand kilometres to go."

"What??"

"Oh wait, that's Sydney, Australia. How come this thing won't talk?"

"Who knows. Call the kids."

"The kids are at work."

"Remind me to call them."

I won't. The kids need a break from frantic phone calls from their father about phones, televisions, cameras, and computers. I'm surprised they still answer their phones.

At least when we're driving down the highway I get to listen to the radio, which is something I never do when I'm writing. Getting caught up on all the CBC programs that used to bore me to tears when my father played them in his car. When did I become him?

The only time I really hate driving on the highway is going through Montreal or Toronto. I've been known to cover my head with a blanket or sweater. How that's going to help me in a crash, I'll never know, but I feel better when I can't see what's happening.

Lately, I've started to cover my head while watching the news, for the same reason.

FIVE HUNDRED YEARS

"/"

IT'S BEEN FIVE HUNDRED YEARS SINCE MARCH 15, 2020.

Hubby and I spend an hour every morning discussing what to have for supper, since it's our only excitement for the day.

I have spring cleaned and decluttered my entire house from top to bottom over and over again...in my mind.

To date I've seen 2,300,000 murders on Netflix. There was an annoying character on the screen last night and I actually said out loud, "Just slit his throat and be done with it."

And now I'm suffering from Netflix eye strain. It's my only exercise.

There was a goose in the field one morning standing on one leg. I raced home and googled why.

When we hear our computer sound the notification ding for pictures of our precious granddaughter, hubby and I have been known to push each other out of the way to get to the screen first. She's only three months old and it's been five hundred years since we've seen her in person!

I made the mistake of hearing a health expert say what you should clean in your house during these difficult times. He mentioned vacuuming your mattress. Like I don't have enough to fret about, what with murdering wasps on the horizon.

People tell me during this pandemic I have lots of time to write another book.

Piss off and leave me alone. I have a family-sized bag of M&M's to finish.

THE TRIP HOME

"**/**"

O NE OF THE NICE THINGS ABOUT GOING INTO TOWN FOR AN EXERCISE CLASS EVERY morning is that I get to go to the grocery store before I go home.

This doesn't sound significant, but when you live in the country and happen to run out of something, you can't walk to the corner shop, or even drive a couple of minutes to a convenience store. It can be more than an hour-long ordeal between driving there, shopping for a few minutes, and coming back, so most of the time I just turn the page and move on to a new recipe that doesn't require the ingredient I don't have.

Of course, the trouble with running into Sobeys for only a few groceries every day is that I always spy a couple of extra things as I rush down the aisles. When I only need milk and bread, I'll see a package of asparagus on sale and throw it in the cart. Ditto for Greek yogurt and baby spinach. My few things have now cost me forty-six dollars. Multiply that by five days of the week, and it adds up.

Going to the store for a few things used to cost twenty dollars not so long ago. I'm old enough to remember when it cost ten dollars, and even five. I clearly recall the day in 1967 when my mother made several trips from the car to bring in a week worth of groceries. She plunked the last of them down on the kitchen table with a gigantic sigh.

"Thirty-five dollars! Can you imagine?"

So today I ran in for tomato sauce, mozzarella cheese, and black olives to make, you guessed it, a pizza. A Weight Watchers pizza. The kind hubby won't touch because it's got black olives on it. I know this, so that's why I stick them on there, so I can have some left over for tomorrow night's supper as well. (Don't judge me. He's barbecuing his honkin' steak.)

It was while I was heading for the tomato sauce aisle that I quickly veered down the fruit aisle instead, in the hopes of scoring something interesting for breakfast besides dreary bananas. Lo and behold, the aproned fruit guy was placing brand new, fat to almost bursting cantaloupes on the shelf, two for five dollars. What?! Normally these suckers cost $6.99 each.

I paused for a second, because having two ginormous cantaloupes in the fridge is cause for alarm as far as elbow room goes, but what the heck. Now they're in my cart.

When I got back to my new keyless car (which is still unnerving), two big trucks had parked on either side of me, so I didn't have a lot of space to open my car doors. I was left to put my few groceries in the trunk of the car, which I normally never do, unless we're on a Costco run in Halifax. And the reason why I never do is because of what happened next.

I was stopped at the traffic light as I was leaving the parking lot, and the minute the light turns green, I made a sharp left turn towards home.

THUNK, THUNK, THUNK.

My massive cantaloupes decided to escape their flimsy bag and careen like bowling balls to the right. Drat! Now I was stuck in traffic, or at least Glace Bay's idea of traffic, and I had to carry on up the main drag. I hoped it wouldn't be so bad, but before long another corner had to be negotiated, and this one is ninety degrees. My renegade tropical fruit specimens were now ping-ponging to all four corners of the trunk.

There was obviously only one solution to this problem. Pull over, get out of the car, open the trunk, put the darn things back in the bag, and place them on the passenger seat. But did I do that? No. Of course not. I watched a program on television once that said you should never get out of the car on the side of the road in case you get clipped by oncoming vehicles. Of course, thinking about it now, they were probably talking about driving in Los Angeles or New York, and not on a lonely rural road in Homeville, Cape Breton.

All I did was curse under my breath and make a face every time I heard a whack.

The cantaloupes became giant dimpled golf balls. I managed to cut a few firm pieces away, but the rest was relegated to the blender for smoothies, and quite frankly cantaloupe smoothies are pathetic.

Like me.

LAUNDROMAT ADVENTURES

"**/**"

T HERE ARE TWO KINDS OF PEOPLE IN THE WORLD. THOSE WHO KNOW WHAT TO DO IN a laundromat and those who don't have a clue.

I haven't stepped inside a laundromat in years, and so anything I might have known is now long gone. It's a scary adventure and quite nerve-wracking, because you may get there and every washer and dryer is being used, and for some reason, you feel as though these people knew you were coming today and ran to throw their clothes in the washers ahead of you, just to be mean.

Scowling at people doesn't do any good, because you never know if you're going to need their goodwill later that afternoon.

My promise to myself was that I was going to wash all the blankets and quilts in the cottage before summer arrived. We've accumulated a lot of them over the past fifty years, especially old wool ones that no one likes anymore. But I can't throw them out, even though they're itchy and uncomfortable, because I remember my grandmother laying them out in the field in the sunshine, or out on the line, and just don't have to heart to throw them in a bin bag. They've served us faithfully over the years. And you can't deny that they keep you warm.

But some of my quilts are too big for my machine, so I trooped into the laundromat with four of them, destined for the two super-duper washing machines in this particular establishment. I looked at them and blinked. There were a lot of instructions and two slots that indicated quarters and loonies. Foolishly, I asked a woman dealing with a mountain of clothes of her own how much I had to put in and if I could use toonies.

She pointed at the slots. "It says quarters and loonies, so you can't use toonies."

The woman who ran the joint hollered from her counter where she was folding clothes. "You can't use toonies, my love. I've got change." Imagine being nice to me even though I was clearly a moron.

Once I had my loonies, I went back to the machine and realized I didn't know how much to put in. "Sorry," I said to the woman still dealing with her own haul, "how much are these washers?"

"Six dollars."

"Six dollars?!" That seemed a bit much.

"But you can get a lot in them."

I was planning on putting only one quilt in each washer, but quickly changed my mind and ending up squishing two quilts in each machine.

Now I had to figure out where to put the laundry detergent. It had a diagram that I didn't pay much attention to, but I did notice that there were spaces for detergent, fabric softener, bleach, etc. I'd forgotten these extras. I poured in a lot of liquid to make sure that the quilts got enough soap, and then spent the next twenty-four minutes terrified that the soap was going to start coming out of the top of the machine, based on the completely sudsy windows on the two front-loaders. There were beads of sweat on my upper lip as I waited for the rinse cycle to kick in, because my windows continued to look like a bubble bath on crack. Oh rats. I was going to have to do this twice.

Surprisingly, by the time the cycles ended and I held the quilts in my hands, they seemed to be soap free.

Just then another woman came in and filled up most of the dryers. There were two left. I put two quilts in one dryer and two in another. "Excuse me. How much are the dryers?"

"A quarter for three minutes."

Three minutes? "And how long do you need to dry the clothes?"

"I usually need an hour."

An hour? So, if you need a quarter for three minutes, how many minutes in an hour? Sixty, I think, so sixty divided by three is...twenty, so twenty times twenty-five is...no wait...I only need twenty quarters, so how much is twenty quarters? Four quarters is a dollar, so that makes ten dollars...no it doesn't...that's five dollars, right? I only had two quarters in my change purse, so I put quarters in the machine to start it before I asked for a motherlode of change, but nothing happened. I looked again. There was a sign. "Not working."

Great. Now I had to switch the clothes to another dryer. But someone had snapped it up while I was counting money in my head.

Nuts to this. I'll take my four damp quilts home and throw them in my own dryer one at a time, or hang them on the line, or spread them over a couple of chairs in the basement.

Hauling four damp quilts is quite a workout. Especially when one of the garbage bag rips open because it's so heavy, and everything ends up falling on the dirty pavement beside the car.

It will be another fifty years before I do that again.

I'VE GOT A SECRET

"I"

I'VE GOT A SECRET, BUT I CAN'T TELL YOU WHAT IT IS. BY THE TIME THIS IS PUBLISHED, it might be common knowledge, but until then I have to keep this news to myself.

And it's KILLING ME!

When someone tells you a secret, you feel honoured and privileged that they trust you with this information, but the minute they leave the room, it's like you have a huge yoke around your neck. How am I supposed to walk the earth knowing what I know and not do anything about it? Not tell someone else? Not share it?

Now you wish the person hadn't said anything because they've given you this huge responsibility, and if it ever gets out, then they are going to know darn well who leaked it. All fingers would point in your direction, and rightly so.

This is too much pressure. But why? Why does knowing a secret suddenly make you feel like your head is going to explode if you don't get it off your chest?

Then again, not all people have this immature reaction. What about wartime spies? Everyday heroes who kept their mouths shut and saved us all. When I think of them, I feel like a pathetic, snivelling coward, but that doesn't mean I don't still want to run up to someone and take them by the shoulders and shake them back and forth. "Guess what I know?! Can you guess?!"

Wanting to tell someone a secret is like wanting to cheat on a diet. You know you shouldn't. You know you'll hate yourself the minute you put that big bite of chocolate brownie in your mouth. The pleasure it will bring will last ten seconds at most, and then you'll have remorse for the rest of the day. It would be the same thing if I spill the beans about my secret. I wouldn't have held up my end of the bargain.

People assume that those of us who can't keep a secret have no self-control. And I'm sad to say that sounds about right. I've kept a few secrets in my lifetime, but only for my own self-preservation. There's nothing noble about me.

Hubby, on the other hand, is like a locked safe if you tell him a secret. My cousin Barbara told him something once in confidence when we were first married, over forty years ago. It wasn't that long ago that she told me about it, assuming I knew.

"I didn't know that!"

"You didn't?"

'No!"

"But I told John. I assumed he told you."

"Barb, did you tell John not to say anything to anyone?"

"Yes."

"Well, that was your first mistake."

"Wow. Imagine that. Someone who keeps their word."

While I admire people who can keep a secret, they're sort of irritating, too. They make you feel bad about yourself. No, I take that back. They don't make you feel anything. *You* make you feel bad, because you know you're not as worthy as they are.

Hubby knows this secret too, and he's as quiet as a mouse. I don't see him itching to tell anyone. He's quite content to let the matter marinate for as long as it should, while I'm behind him pulling my hair out.

It's a good thing no one has ever sent me behind enemy lines. I'd be crowing like a rooster the minute they tie me up and shine a big light on my face.

"Where's the rendezvous taking place?"

"In the Costco parking lot, but who cares! I'm going to be a grandmother!!!!"

KEEPSAKES

"**/**"

F IRST OF ALL, I LOVE THE WORD *KEEPSAKE*. YOU ARE KEEPING SOMETHING FOR YOUR own sake. It means something to you. It brings you pleasure just looking at it. And it can be anything. You can't judge someone else's keepsake, because its meaning is pointless to everyone else. That's why you get to keep it. For your own sake.

Most of my keepsakes are from the natural world. I have tiny tins, woven baskets, jewelry boxes and jars filled with rocks, feathers, twigs, bird nests, bird eggs, shells, birchbark, and a small wasps' nest. My eagle feather was a miraculous find, as was a piece of driftwood shaped exactly like a whale. I have a heart-shaped stone I found on the beach one day, and a very small old-fashioned key that opens something mysterious, lost in time.

The best keepers of keepsakes are old-fashioned cookie or candy tins. You definitely need a tight lid to keep your treasures in and away from a sibling's prying eyes. I remember once my grandmother let me pick some buttons out of her sewing basket, and I kept them for years. My sister was sure I'd taken the best ones. (I had.)

Why do we all love pockets? It's not just for tissues. We need a pouch to pick something up and take it with us. Humans love to collect things. We obviously love to be buried with things too. The mighty had vast fortunes around them when they died. But throughout history, even the lowliest and insignificant souls, according to the outside world, were buried with tokens made by loved ones.

We do the same things with our beloved pets. They are always buried in a favourite ratty blanket, with their best toy snuggled in beside them. We need to know that they are not alone.

What you keep says a lot about you. If you wandered through my dusty house, the first thing you'd notice is that I have many animals in every room in my house. That's because animals are my favourite things in the whole world. The last time I went to England, I came home with a stuffed toy fox wearing a jaunty plaid waistcoat, looking like a British country gentleman. He sits in a rocking chair.

My mother knitted a toy mouse for one of the kids when they were born. I forget which, but that mouse is one of my prized possessions. A lot of women collect purses or shoes, but my money is always spent on frogs or hippos or owls.

Everyone knows about my passion. I had a neighbour who loved to go hunting. Despite this, I actually liked the guy. One Christmas, I sent them a card with reindeer on the cover, and I wrote in big letters, "Do not shoot, Alan!" He loved that card.

That's another thing I keep. Cards with funny sayings, or great cartoons. I received one recently from a great pal, a minister. It shows Jesus on his cellphone, looking at Twitter. "Twelve followers so far. Sweet." It made me smile for days.

I was smart enough to keep all my daughter's drawings over the years. She'd sit in front of *Mr. Dressup* every day and do artwork. I thought her pictures of animals were amazing, and I have them up on the walls to this day. She became a talented graphic designer. (She designed the logo for the Halifax Hurricanes basketball team, and she'll kill me for mentioning this.)

Recipes are another keepsake of mine, even though I rarely make anything new. I just like knowing they're available. I love collecting old church-group recipe books from the fifties and sixties. Great stodgy, calorie-laden concoctions made by a Mrs. Bill Smith. Now we all know that Bill probably couldn't make a meal to save his life, so it irks me that he is given the credit, when it should've been his wife who claimed the glory. But we'll never know her name because of the social mores of the time.

Life is just better when we keep something personal for ourselves. I try to remember that when hubby drags home yet another old Pepsi bottle he found buried in the woods, now soaking in soapy water in our kitchen sink.

"That's disgusting! Who knows what kind of germs are in that!"

"To each his own, my dear."

Yeah, right.

I'M SINKING

"I"

D ON'T YOU ABSOLUTELY LONG FOR THE DAYS WHEN WE HAD FEWER OPTIONS ABOUT everything? In today's world, we are literally drowning in choices, and I seriously think it's affecting our mental health. I know it's affecting mine.

I can't think anymore.

When we were kids, our mom would take us to Woolworth's to sit on the diner stools and twirl around before she shopped. She'd order coffee. That's all she had to say. It would arrive. We were given the choice of a chocolate, vanilla, or strawberry milkshake. My grandmother would decide between a slice of apple, cherry, or lemon meringue pie.

That was it! It was simple and yet so good.

Now it's heart palpitations when I try and order a coffee, because it's not my mother's coffee, is it? It's an expresso or a latte or something with pumpkin-spiced whipped cream on top. Nowadays I feel guilty if I don't ask for coffee that's ethically sourced. Did you know that you can ask for Kopi Luwak coffee that's $160–$600 a pound, or what about Thai Arabica coffee that's naturally refined by elephants? It goes by another name: elephant-poop coffee. You can find it next to the bat-poop coffee.

Have you tried choosing a pair of glasses lately? There are literally millions of choices in the stores or online. How do you pick one? When I was a kid, we had two choices. Ugly and less ugly. I'm not suggesting we go back to that. I'm just saying that it's very difficult to pick something when you know that the minute you buy it, you're going to see a pair on someone else that are absolutely stunning, and suddenly your new glasses look second-rate.

What about getting a dog? Dogs used to be mutts. They followed you home and you took them in. They were free for the taking, and absolutely scruffy and adorable. Now we have designer dogs that cost a flipping fortune. Those in the know now want little French Bulldogs because they're the most popular canines at the moment. Granted, they are incredibly sweet, but so is the ratty-looking specimen waiting longingly for someone to pick him from behind the wire cage at the pound.

You decide you want to veg in front of the telly on Saturday night, so you go to Netflix and spend an hour trying to pick between an American gangster movie, a British spy thriller, a Russian military drama, an Italian mob series, or a troubling Norwegian film noire. There are so many movies with guns and violence and zombies that I usually give up. Although there was a Swiss documentary on neutrality and the benefits of dark chocolate that looked interesting. [Author's note. This was obviously written before the pandemic. I'm a murder expert now.]

These days, when I go to a restaurant and look through the fifteen pages of menu options, I feel the need to take an Ativan.

But the biggest minefield has to be the cosmetic industry. There are so many products for a woman's skin now that if she used all of them, her face would melt away in the mirror. It used to be that you were told to wash your face with soap and if you had to, smear on Pond's Cold Cream or Noxzema. Then out the door you went.

Now you lather with a non-drying gel or exfoliant product before dabbing on toner, and then finger on essential serum before applying your moisturizer, and don't forget that your sunscreen goes on next, and lastly your liquid foundation, which is sealed in with loose translucent powder before you even start to apply your make-up.

And every cosmetic company screeches that their products are the newest, the best, the boldest, the freshest, the safest, the hippest, the hottest, the dewiest...on and on and on.

We are so bombarded with choice that's it's all starting to run together, like when you mix lovely colours in a jar. You reach a tipping point where the water just turns a murky, unappetizing grey.

We don't need everything.

HUMMING AND SINGING

"/"

I T'S BEEN BROUGHT TO MY ATTENTION THAT I HUM A LOT, BUT I DIDN'T REALIZE THIS was annoying to those in my inner circle.

I do know that the minute I get in an elevator, I hum. Then I glance at hubby and he's smirking at me. Depending on my mood, I will stop instantly, turn away from him and keep humming, or stick my tongue out at him.

My humming is not mindless. I hum Broadway show tunes from the good old days, like *Oklahoma*: "Oh, what a beautiful morning! Oh, what a beautiful day! I've got a beautiful feeling, everything's going my way!" And of course, "Shall We Dance," from *The King and I*. Most of the time I know the melody but not all the words, which is why I hum. But I also sing spontaneously. I usually belt out the entire score of *The Sound of Music* when I cook supper or change the kitty litter.

But the one that gets everyone's attention is "I wanna be where the people are. I wanna see, wanna see 'em dancin'..." I burst into this song regularly at the kitchen sink or while doling out ice-cream for the gang. Now my Korean daughter-in-law belts it out while making bibimbap or sushi.

From Disney's *Snow White and the Seven Dwarfs,* "I'm wishing, I'm wishing, for the one I love, to find me, to find me, today. TODAY!" That's another great one.

Why do I insist on humming these tunes for no reason?

It's called self-soothing.

"Self-soothing usually takes place through the senses...enjoyable sensory experiences signal the brain that there is no emergency and everything's going to be okay, i.e., a sound, to sing or hum or listen to a cat's purr... self-soothing is a powerful tool for tolerating distress." Carrie Elizabeth Lin wrote this in June 2015 for Addiction.com.

Apparently, I'm distressed 24/7, and while humming might be soothing to me, it bugs everyone else in my vicinity. Now that I've been forced to recognize it, I'm keeping tabs on where I do it the most. The elevator is an easy one to understand; I hate elevators. The instant I get in one, I imagine some bad guy slicing the cables with a machete, to send us hurtling downward to instant death. When this bad-guy scenario crept into my consciousness, I'll never know.

Humming in cars is fun. "When the red, red robin, comes bob, bob, bobbin' along," or singing my perennial favourite, "Mama's little baby loves shortenin', shortenin', Mama's little baby loves shortenin' bread! Put on the fire, put on the lead, Mama's gonna make some shortenin' bread. And that ain't all, she's goin' to do, Mama's gonna make some cornbread too!"

This ditty makes me instantly happy, and able to endure a long lull in conversation, if you're driving with someone you don't know very well. Or if you're standing in line at Old Navy.

Humming has to be one of the better ways of placating myself, instead of walking around with a weighted blanket over my shoulders, sucking on a soother.

Now that I'm aware of this blip in my personality, I have to be more careful. Once, I hummed "Bat Out of Hell" by Meatloaf in church. Not that any of the elderly ladies around me would have recognized the tune, but still.

The reason humming makes me happy is that I would hum to my babies while they were in my arms, as I rocked them to sleep. To most mothers, this memory is one of pure joy (as long as the babies went to sleep.) That simple vibration as their ears were pressed against my chest must have sounded like a cat purr.

If humming is my only crime, I think I'm good.

HOLD UP

"/"

WE TWO HAD A NICE DAY PLANNED.
A small family reunion in Baddeck, involving three generations of cousins. It had been too long since we were together. You'd think that Baddeck was in China, that's how often we get together, but never mind, it was happening on this day.

"Here's a brilliant idea," I announced to hubby that morning. "We don't want Barb to make us two meals, so let's stop at the Cedar House on the way and get a bite of lunch first."

"Okay."

What? Hubby said yes to stopping for lunch? This is almost unheard of. He has this thing where he'll begrudgingly stop at a fast-food joint or Tim Horton's while we're on the road, and take something with us to eat while we drive, but to stop at an actual restaurant is almost more than he can bear. He just sits there, shaking one leg in anticipation of the waitress giving us our menus, while the entire fleet of trucks we passed are quickly zooming by, getting ahead of us again.

He can't stand wasting time. I used to point out little craft stores on our way to Halifax. "Why don't we run in and look around?"

"We will when I retire."

We have yet to set a big toe in any of these places, and he's been retired for ten years now. Once he starts the car, he's got blinkers on like an old workhorse. His mind is on the destination, and look out, anyone who stands in his way.

So, we started out okay. We drove by the A & K Lick-a-Chick, where my sister's family stopped to have lunch and buy T-shirts, because that's what tourists do when they see this particular joint.

"Oh-oh," hubby muttered.

"What?"

"Construction."

Cars were slowing down in front of us. There was a construction sign warning us of something dire going on up ahead. We were behind a high-sided van, the kind you can't see over. That somehow made things worse.

"Just our luck," he said.

"Oh well, it shouldn't be too long."

I've tried to block out the next forty minutes of our ordeal, because when you sit in a car that's not moving, every minute feels as if it's at least an hour long.

And what makes it excruciatingly worse is having to listen to the man beside you moan about it every thirty seconds.

"Can you believe this?!"

There's no need to reply. He requires no answer in this frame of mind.

"What are these boneheads doing?!"

"Their job."

An annoyed glance is what I got for that remark.

But after the thirty-minute mark, he was right. Even I started to squirm in my seat, because when there is no end in sight on the highway, your bladder urgently reminds you that you shouldn't have downed that large coffee an hour ago.

At least five hundred cars and trucks went by and then there was a bit of a lull.

"Maybe this is it. This has got to be it. There can't possibly be any more cars coming this way."

Nope. After ten seconds of nothing coming, another huge batch started in. And that's how it continued for the entire forty minutes. Like breaking waves, these vehicles just relentlessly kept driving past us.

Hubby kept looking in the rear-view mirrors. "Look at the lineup behind us! As far as the eye can see! What would it be like if the ferry was in?"

While I sighed, he fumed. Of course, roads need to be fixed and sometimes we're inconvenienced, but I had to admit, this was getting a bit ridiculous. Where were all the cars coming from? We were in rural Cape Breton, not Los Angeles.

Just when I was ready to stuff a sock in hubby's mouth, we started to move, very slowly, behind a long line of other irate drivers. After a few miles of passing the slowpokes in the bunch, the exhilaration of boogying down the highway was wondrous.

Suddenly, there it was. I pointed at the Cedar House sign.

"Are you crazy!" hubby shouted. "We can't stop for lunch now! We'll never get there at this rate!"

I was so close.

HOCKEY GAME ETIQUETTE

"/"

EVERYONE WHO KNOWS ME KNOWS I'M NOT A HOCKEY LOVER. THAT'S BECAUSE I TELL people constantly. And yet I am a Screaming Eagles season ticket holder, because hubby likes to go to the games, and for some reason I have to go with him. He tells me I don't have to come. Yeah, right. Do I honestly want that guilt hanging around my neck?

So, I sit in the seats and pretend to watch the game. I have no idea what is going on. It doesn't matter how many times the rules are explained to me, I don't get it and I never will. Hockey is like the game of curling, or geometry. It just doesn't make sense.

While everyone else is paying attention to what's going on at ice level, I watch the humanity around me. I try not to be obvious, but sometimes I'm not successful.

Hubby pokes me in the ribs. "Keep your eyes on the game. The puck could fly up and hit you in the face."

"Hopefully I'd be knocked out."

He ignores me.

What I find fascinating are the people who wander up and down the aisles while the game is going on. There are signs posted warning you against this, for good reason. People can't see the game if you're in the way. And yet, this is consistently ignored, by kids, teenagers, adults, grandmothers, and grumpy old men. No one is immune to this behaviour. What does it say about the human race, if we can't comply with one simple instruction?

Everyone seated grumbles to each other when this happens, and occasionally someone will point out to the offending party that they're in the wrong, but all they get for their efforts is a dirty look, like they're suddenly pond scum. It's not worth it.

Then we have the early and late brigade. They always have seats in the middle of the row. They never arrive in time to sit before the game starts. You are comfortably seated and watching the game (not me), and suddenly a family of five hovers by your aisle, looking for the row number, with hats, coats, purses, pop bottles, canteen food, and plastic horns draped everywhere. You get up and let them all squeeze by you before they suddenly realize they are in the wrong aisle and you have to get up again and let them all troop out.

Just when you settle back down, you have the four guys who need to get out of their seats with three minutes left in the first period so they can go get their beer before everyone else. These same guys come back five minutes into the second period and make you stand again. Repeat at the end of the second period, and more of the same in the third.

I'm not so miserly that I resent getting out of my seat at all. I do realize I am in an arena and people need to get in and out, but what really gets my goat are the people who don't give you a nanosecond to get up. They are literally on top of you before you can move, almost shoving you aside.

Listen, people. I'm an old, fat gal with a bit of arthritis in my knees, and I haven't jumped in decades, so I need a little time to get this body upright. Some people can push their knees to the side and let you pass, but I'm not one of them. What is so urgent that you can't wait two extra seconds to escape? And I'm not talking about little kids here. I've been trampled by little boys in a frenzy to catch a flying T-shirt, and that's okay. They're excited. It's the grouchy-looking dudes who stare at you and say nothing as they push past you. How about an "Excuse me," or "Thanks," as an acknowledgment that I'm alive?

The one thing I do enjoy about the hockey game is getting to know the people who sit around us. After a few years, you recognize the regulars, and it's nice to exchange pleasantries with them. I'm afraid that at this point they all know my difficult relationship with hockey, and yet they don't hold it against me. I get a kick out of how much they seem to enjoy it.

But it's not all doom and gloom. I don't mind shootouts.

"So, if this guy puts it in the net, we win?"

"Not necessarily."

See what I mean? Who can understand this game?

HIDE-AND-SEEK

"**!**"

D O ANY OF YOU KNOW, AT THIS EXACT MOMENT, WHERE YOUR MARRIAGE CERTIFICATE is? If you do, then you are a better human being than I am.

Hubby received some mail from the Quebec government about something, and in the course of having to reply to their request, he had to find his birth certificate. The stars were aligned, because hallelujah, I just happened to know where it was, which was a minor miracle.

While I was rooting through papers in the filing cabinet, I came upon something hubby put in a folder, about what I should do and who I should get in contact with when he dies. That startled me for a moment, but I'm not surprised it was in there. He's always been terribly organized, and this was information about his company pension.

And one of the items they would want is our marriage certificate. Now, I haven't seen that particular piece of paper since the afternoon of June 26, 1976. Did the minister give it to me, or to John after we signed it? I don't remember holding it with my bouquet as I walked back down the aisle.

"John?"

"Yeah?"

"Where's our marriage certificate?"

"I'm assuming it's in the filing cabinet."

"Under what?"

"M for marriage. W for wedding. I. P. for important paper. That's your department."

"It is?"

"So, you're telling me you don't know where you put it?"

A question like this always raises my blood pressure. "Why am I the only one responsible for making sure our marriage certificate is within reach? There are two people in this relationship. This is as much your problem as it is mine."

"Well, you must have put it somewhere."

"I didn't put it anywhere! And even if I did, how am I supposed to remember something that happened forty-three years ago?"

It occurs to me that I don't even know where we got married. It was a church somewhere in his Montreal neighbourhood. This isn't good. I better gather this information now.

"What was the name of the church where we got married?"

"You don't remember? It was St. Paul's."

"Was it Anglican?"

"You know that."

I don't. But I do now, after that reminder.

"What was the address?"

"Forty-fourth Avenue, Lachine. Is there anything else I can tell you? Do you want to know who was there and what we had to eat at the reception?"

"What *did* we have to eat at the reception?"

"Who knows? All I remember is that open bar. God bless your old man."

Our filing cabinet fills me with dread. It's crammed full of documents about everything under the sun, as well as reams of bank statements and insurance policies, but there's not one file in there that has anything to do with a marriage certificate. I'm going to have to go through every single one of those folders, and the thought of it gives me the willies.

This sort of thing could've been prevented. The only wedding presents we received were towels and a roasting pan and a toaster. What I really needed, and what I will give if I'm ever invited to another wedding, was a big Tupperware container or wicker basket that someone bedazzled the life out of, so that it reads:

Important Papers You Will Need Forty-Three Years from Now!!

I'm starting the clock, to see how long this marriage-certificate game of hide-and-seek is going to last, and I'll report back when it is found. If you never hear from me again, know that I have either gone mad with frustration or left the country under an assumed name.

Miss Jane Doe. I'll be single, because I don't have any proof I was ever married.

P.S. Gave up and paid $47 for the Quebec government to send me another one. You watch. I'll find the original tomorrow.

THE HEAT!!!

" **/** "

NOW I REMEMBER WHY I DON'T LIVE IN THE GOBI DESERT. OR ARIZONA. OR SAUDI Arabia.

Because I melt in the heat. I've been happily living in Cape Breton for most of my life, smug in the knowledge that we have some lovely days, but for the most part, we're used to foggy, misty, damp, cool days that are accompanied by ocean breezes, chilly nights, and average temperatures. A blazing hot day is an anomaly. We can endure it, because we know in six hours a hurricane will blow through or a snowstorm will descend.

But *weeks* of hot, sunny weather is turning me into a person I don't want to know. I whine constantly, and drip. My hair is always wet underneath after the least effort. Having three showers a day is not unheard of.

People who worship the sun must be having a field day, and I'm happy for parents who can get their kids to the beach and create lovely memories, but at this time of my life, I'm like my elderly cat. He's flaked out under the kitchen table on his back, trying to catch his breath from the slight breeze coming in through the crack in the bottom of the screen door. I'm lying with him, hoping no one pops in for a visit.

When you walk around in a lather of sweat, you suddenly become acutely aware of all the places on your body where skin meets skin. Sticking to yourself is very uncomfortable, and now that talcum powder causes cancer, according to screaming court cases, I'm very loath to dust myself, as tempting as it is.

Stupidly, eight years ago, I made the mistake of renovating our kitchen.

In the process, I was determined to take down the two ugly light fixtures with fans attached, for a more stylish design without fans. Hubby has never forgotten this travesty, and any time I mention how hot I am while I boil potatoes, I know what's coming.

"You got rid of the fans."

I point my potato masher at him. "No! You want mashed potatoes!"

"If we had a fan, you wouldn't be so hot, so it's your fault. You took down those perfectly good fans and now you're suffering."

Technically, he's right, but bringing it up constantly is a dangerous thing to do.

Hot weather curtails activities in our house.

"Let's go to a movie."

"On a day like this? Are you crazy?"

"But it might be nice to sit in a darkened, air-conditioned area for a couple of hours."

"Never!" hubby declares. "It's against the law to go to the movies on a hot day."

"Is it also against the law to go to a nice restaurant?"

"That's even worse! You can't eat out when you can barbeque at home in the blazing heat!"

Nothing out of the ordinary can be done on a nice day. You need to be outside. This is a throwback to our growing-up years in the fifties and sixties, when mothers shooed you outside with their brooms and didn't want to see you again until suppertime.

But surely, the world is changing, because it's too hot to ride bikes for hours without risking sunstroke or seizures. Even news reports tell you when a heat wave is about to descend and the order is given for you to stay indoors.

We are creatures of habit, and during the winter months, all we do is moan about the cold and wish for the summer sunshine. But when it comes day after day and you can fry eggs on sidewalks, it's not quite as wonderful as we remember.

It was so hot yesterday that when friends showed up at the bungalow and ran to give me a big hug of hello, I had to ward them off with my arms outstretched. "Don't touch me! I'm sweaty!" There is nothing worse than giving someone a hug and finding out too late they are a damp sausage. So, we did the Hollywood thing and air-kissed and pretended to pat each others' shoulders.

THE HEAT!!!

The best thing in the world at this time of year is an air-conditioned automobile. When you crawl into a molten car that's been sitting in a parking lot for a couple of hours, you desperately scramble to get the a/c working pronto, and when it finally awakens with a genuine blast of Arctic air, it's a feeling like no other.

The next time we go to town, and who knows when that will be—"We can't go to town on a hot day!"—I'll admit my foolishness and buy a light fixture for the kitchen with a fan on it. I don't care what designer shows say. I have no friends, so no one comes to our house, and it will be just hubby and I and the cat enjoying the ugly fan immensely.

OLD CATS

"/"

I'VE DECIDED THAT OLD CATS ARE LIKE SOME OLD PEOPLE: INCREDIBLY DEMANDING OF attention. This is not a criticism. I'm an old woman, incredibly demanding of attention, so I know one when I see one.

Our elderly cat, Pip, has decided the best spot in the house is to be draped over my left arm as I type at my computer. He's on me now, purring, just to make me feel guilty if I try to remove him.

This is a relatively new phenomenon, and at first it was endearing, but now it's becoming a pain in the wrist. Every single time I walk into my study and sit in my chair, he appears instantly from another part of the house and jumps on the bed and then walks around the furniture until he sticks out a paw to reach the edge of my desk, and like a fool, I bring it closer to him, because he is elderly and I don't want him to fall to the floor.

Then he lies on me like a dead weight and doesn't move until I can't stand it and have to wiggle my now very warm and furry arm out from under him, all the while saying to myself, "You're going to miss this when he's gone, so you better appreciate it now," which makes me feel wretched.

It's the same feeling I used to get when my kids were little and they wanted to "help" me at the sink, so they'd scrape a chair across the kitchen floor and stand on it and essentially shove me out of the way, splashing water and soap everywhere, while looking at me with such glee that I'd smile and let them do it, even though I wanted to push them off the chair and tell them to leave me alone.

Pip has also started to walk ahead of us at a snail's pace every time we walk down our hallway. It's like a little parade every time we want to get to the kitchen or bathroom or bedroom. Not only that, he purr-meows every three seconds while doing it. He's like a heat-seeking missile looking for his target. We can't go anywhere without his approval. A small and furry crossing-guard, afraid we're going to get hurt if we walk to the linen closet.

But he's so slow! I've almost killed myself several times trying not to trip over him. He's like that miserable snail-paced driver in front of you when you're late for an appointment. No amount of huffing or puffing makes him move, so you end up pulling your hair out and swearing, to no avail.

This behaviour has come about because he misses his brother. It doesn't matter that he picked on him his whole life, now that Neo is gone, it's lonely in the house without him. I understand that. The kids left long ago, but sometimes I feel lost and I'd love to have them come home and pat me on the head, or let me follow them around wherever they're going.

I do have a kinship with this cat, and recognize his neediness at this point in his life, but being the one he's decided he can't live without is a strain. It's getting to the point where I'm avoiding my desk, which is playing havoc with this column-writing gig. But how can I shut the door in Pip's face so I can get some work done? I can feel his Puss-in-Boots eyes boring into the back of my skull. What is it with mothers and guilt??

And don't say he's just a cat. A cat is never just a cat to the people who love him. And if I don't tolerate this behaviour, I will sorely regret it when he goes to his great catnip reward in the sky. I can already feel his warm presence on my arm, even when he's not on it.

Please let that last.

GUILTY PLEASURE

"**|**"

AS PART OF MY EXERCISE ROUTINE, (THAT SOUNDS MORE IMPRESSIVE THAN IT IS), I use a recumbent bike we have in our basement/family room/storage area. It's always ice-cold down there, but I soon warm up trying to get my old knees to move out of first gear.

In this marvellous room, which houses my daughter's entire collection of Beanie Babies, which she refuses to take to her house, there's an old television. It weighs three thousand pounds, so it's not going anywhere, and the fact that it's still working is sort of fantastic. There are ten remotes in a basket, and so far, I've figured out which one turns the television on and off, but that's it. I can't turn the channel. The button is stuck and I can't bear to ask hubby what's wrong, because he'll come down and try to explain it to me, and I don't have that kind of time.

So, for forty minutes every day, I've been watching TLC. Just recently I found out the initials stand for The Learning Channel, if you can believe that. I thought it was Tender Loving Care, or at least The Lousy Channel, because the shows are beyond ridiculous.

With one exception. I've always watched *Say Yes to the Dress*, mainly because I have a daughter and you get to fantasize about your own little girl while you're watching it, dabbing your eyes at all the mother/daughter moments.

But lately I've watched an episode of *Long Island Medium*, the loud, chatty woman with fingernails that could decapitate you if you got close enough. She's forever buying a sandwich and biting her lip before asking the

131

waitress if her mom is dead. The she proceeds to tell the woman that her mother's feet used to hurt and she used to make doilies. The waitress bursts into tears and confirms that's her mother to a tee. They hug and off she goes, to tell the guy pumping her gas that his grandfather is standing behind him with a fedora on his head. The gas guy can't believe it and wipes away tears.

Now I'm dying to meet this woman! Can it be true? I'll have to keep watching.

The other morning, I turned it on to discover it was a show about hoarding. Merciful God. I'm Martha Stewart compared to these poor people. Naturally, I was prepared to harden my heart against this man because he was clearly insane, but then the therapist took him to an antique store and asked him to pick out two things he'd like. He chose two old bottles, only about four inches tall. They were *fantastic*. She made him walk out of the store without them, the heartless cow.

Last week I watched thirty minutes of a show called *My 600-Lb Life*. I was in tears by the end of it. These are my people, because I understand their frustration, and easing their anxiety with food. Who among us hasn't roared into the Tasty-Treat drive-through after work when the boss yelled at us? Or picked up an entire wheel of brie and put it in the back of the fridge, so no one else can find it? Oh. That's probably just me.

Today I watched an advertisement for a new show that's going to debut on TLC. I forget the name of it, but the premise is, a woman named Pooh goes to a guy's house and tells the poor schmuck he can't rap, and if he doesn't stop trying to make it into the "rap" music business, his wife is going to leave him.

Why can't the wife just tell the guy herself? Why get Pooh involved? What are Pooh's credentials, anyway? My only option is to keep watching to find out.

Then there's *Tattoo Girls* and a show called *Secret Princes*. Now, I haven't managed to catch these yet, but I'm assuming one show is about girls tattooing people and the other is about a group of princes (how many can there possibly be?) wandering around the United States, with secrets they can't tell anyone.

Fascinating.

NEW VS. OLD

"**!**"

AS I SIT HERE TWISTING THE SKIN TAGS ON MY NECK, I REALIZE THIS IS A NEW anxiety behaviour in my repertoire, now that I can't bite my fingernails. (DON'T TOUCH YOUR FACE.)

I've also been shredding paper. Not manually, but perhaps I should. While I was happily killing address labels on old envelopes, I smelled burnt toast. It always happens. You finally get around to impersonating Marie Kondo and your helper sets itself on fire.

While I returned hubby's birthday shirts, I bought a new paper shredder. And lo and behold, I read the instruction manual because this is what you do when you're moping around the house, thanks to COVID-19. It said I can only use it for two minutes at a time?? Unbelievable! No wonder my old one decided life wasn't worth living.

You apparently have to let it rest for thirty minutes between the two-minute cutting sessions?! Did you know this? Bloody hell. So now I'm creeping downstairs at various intervals during the day to shred for 120 seconds at a time. It's like sneaking around trying to have a cigarette.

Back in the day, they made things to last at least twenty thousand years. Ask any archaeologist. And I don't have to go that far back. The fridges and stoves of my grandmother and mother's vintage were all perfectly good when they threw them out because they wanted a new "stylish" model, an avocado green or harvest gold number.

We have an old Frigidaire fridge in the shed at the bungalow that still works, but because it's environmentally unfriendly, it sits there bored out of its mind. I don't have the heart to throw it out, since it would happily hum away if you asked it to. It can't help it if the world has moved on to new standards.

Maybe I've harped on this before, but I have my mother's kitchen utensil set that hangs from a delicate steel bar with hooks that you put on the wall. It was a wedding present when Mom and Dad got married in 1950, so that makes it seventy years old. The utensils are heavy and well-made and look brand new. So brand new you could put them in a box and re-gift them and no one would be the wiser. But there is no way anyone is getting their mitts on these babies. They are my prized possessions. My evidence that we've lost the art of craftsmanship.

What a pity.

GOSSIP

"**/**"

FORGET THE INTERNET.

You can find out the juiciest gossip just leaning into the window of a car door. When you live in a rural community, the best stories are exchanged when you happen to be out walking and your neighbour passes you on their way to work. They slow down and the intel begins.

How much you receive depends on the time of year. During blackfly season, you're usually out of luck as to hearing what's happening with your neighbours down the laneway, because thirty seconds into the conversation, either you or the driver inhales one of the little buggers and coughing ensues.

But if you have a good day, the stories are endless.

"Did ya hear that widower down the road is getting married again?"

"Are you serious?"

"Swear to God."

Now the trouble with exchanges like this is that the gossip and the receiver are not talking about the same person. The gossip is talking about the old coot who's been alone for ten years. The listener thinks the gossiper is talking about the young coot, who only buried his wife a month ago.

In the space of a day and a half, every person collecting their mail on your mail route will think that the young coot is a miserable so-and-so, and give him dirty looks when he's outside mowing his grass.

Then there's the soon-to-be grandmother who rolls down her window to tell you that the baby is a boy! You yell, "Hurrah! Congratulations!" and continue with your stroll. Then you go home and tell hubby that Cinderella had her baby. You both run into Cinderella a few weeks later and tell her how happy you are about her baby. She looks at her big bump.

"I haven't had it yet."

You forget that people can know the sex of their baby months beforehand. You really must get with the times.

A great topic of conversation happens when someone is selling their house. Everyone in the community is invested in this.

"How much do you think they'll get for it?"

"Girl, not enough to buy a house anywhere else."

"Ain't that the truth."

Which is why we'll never be moving to the city.

Bumping into people is when you get the lowdown on someone's health. The grocery aisle is the perfect place to ask impossibly personal questions.

"How's your husband?"

"Not good. Not good at all."

"Oh dear, what's wrong?"

"He was in a lot of pain and they opened him up, but when they sewed him together again, I think they did it too tight because now his feet are acting up. On top of that, the poor man has terrible gas."

Does this poor soul know his wife is a blabbermouth? But that doesn't stop you from asking more questions. "Didn't he have a heart attack a while back?"

"Yes! From watchin' the friggin' lotto! He thought he won, but it turns out he missed the jackpot by one number."

When you run into the mothers of the kids that your kids knew at school a decade ago, you get their entire life story in a matter of minutes. It can go two ways.

"Junior's a test pilot and after travelling the world, he married a member of the British royal family. Their triplets are due soon."

You're suddenly really anxious about your own kids.

Or...

"Well, our Angel went to community college, but she hated that, so she had a baby and went to Fort McMurray with her boyfriend, but he turned out to be a louse and her father was after almost killin' the fool, so she came back home and now we're looking after our granddaughter and Angel's pregnant again, God love her, and she's working at the mall, but she's talking about moving to Florida with her new man, but her dad's not keen on that because he's covered with tattoos, but I told him you're only young once and let her live a little, and he said she's lived a little too much as far as he's concerned, but you know daddies and their little girls."

You're suddenly really happy about your own kids.

GOING GAGA

O KAY, SO ASK ME WHERE I WAS ON JANUARY 26, 2019.
My adventure starts on a very cold morning, when I arrive at my appointment to have my chin hairs zapped. My gal is hanging out her front door.

"Call hubby! It's important."

Oh, dear God. Who died? I fumble with my cellphone and punch in our number. "What????!!"

"WHY DO YOU NEVER HAVE THAT BLASTED PHONE ON?"

"Stop yelling at me! Who died?"

"You need to call Deborah right away."

Deborah is a dear friend who lives in Ohio. "Oh God! Who died in Ohio?!"

"No one is dead. Just call her."

Okay. This is weird. I can call Deborah whenever I want, but why is she trying to track me down on a boring winter morning? I call her. "What's wrong?"

"Listen carefully. It's my sixtieth birthday..."

"Have you lost your mind? You're calling to tell me it's your birthday? You nearly gave me a heart attack!"

"Stop talking. I need your answer now. Can you jump on a plane and fly to Las Vegas to see Lady Gaga? Your plane reservation, front-row-seat concert ticket, and luxury hotel are all paid for. Just say yes or no."

Now, things like this don't usually happen to me. Not when I'm standing in the freezing cold with a hairy chin. I babble for a moment, my eyes glazing over.

It would be churlish to decline.

"O.M.G. YES!"

I'm the luckiest person alive!

The very next day I am sick as a dog and crying in my bed. "Can you believe this?! I'm SICK! I can't get on a plane!"

Hubby packs my bag, makes me chug cold medicine, and shoves Kleenex in my pocket. "Have a great time."

This lump of misery flies across North America by herself, peering down at the bright lights of the Vegas Strip from the airplane window, with my itchy, watery, red eyes. I'm hunched over, getting into the taxi. If this guy decides to drive me into the desert, I really don't care.

Deborah doesn't know that I'm under the weather, so she greets me at the hotel with a shocked look. "What happened to you?"

The waterworks start. "I'm sick! But I'm going to have a great time, I swear!"

She orders room service. Tea with honey and lemon. I look at the bill and shriek. "Eighteen American dollars!"

She grabs it out of my hand. "What happens in Vegas, stays in Vegas. Now go to bed."

I am a country mouse in this world. A snivelling, anxious, achy mouse, who has now seen things that cannot be unseen. Let's just say, I will never worry about what I wear again.

It's all a blur of fantastic food, cocktails, poolside relaxation, and then the concert.

Our seats are next to the stage. I mean, really? I have to wipe my teary eyes to believe what I'm seeing next. There's a bit of a commotion a few feet away to the left, and then suddenly, there's Bradley Cooper, sitting in a seat with his ball cap on backwards. We can reach out and touch him if we have a mind to. He's here to cheer on Lady Gaga.

We watch the concert in awe. Her voice is simply amazing. It fills the entire theatre. It's so amazing that I stop sniffing and coughing and shout and dance with everyone else. Then she says she has a wonderful friend in the audience and wonders if he'd come up and sing with her. The place goes nuts when Bradley Cooper gets up and sings a duet, their song "Shallow" from the movie *A Star Is Born*.

This guy is as handsome as he seems on the screen. You really do get star-struck when you see someone that good-looking in front of you. If it wasn't for my lousy cold, I would have hopped over my seat and given him a Cape Breton hug, my hairless chin beaming in the strobe lights. Alas, he'll never have the pleasure of that embrace.

The next night, I catch the red-eye from Sin City and cough my way back to Toronto and then Sydney. Hubby is there to collect me at the airport. He puts me to bed and I fall into a deep slumber.

Eventually, I shuffle into the kitchen. Hubby is at the table on his computer.

"How are you feeling?"

"Gaga."

THE LONE RANGER

"I"

ONE OF THE MOST DIFFICULT ASPECTS OF THIS MOMENT IN TIME IS NOT KNOWING who you're running into, because people wearing masks all look the same. But even with masks, some of us are more stylish than others. I'm definitely in the snooze category, with my black Lone Ranger mask. I have others, but I tend to grab the black one. Someone once said that black is slimming. I doubt they meant over your jawline, when the rest of your body sticks out like a sore thumb down below, but I'll go with that conventional wisdom.

So, I'm wandering around Walmart the other day, picking up stocking stuffers in one fell swoop so I don't have to go near a store in December when the crowds are sure to be worse. I say *wandering* because I'm trying to follow the arrows and go the right way, which tends to make me cover more area than I want to, but rules are rules and I'm nothing if not a coward, so I make sure no one has any reason to yell at me.

But soon my Spidey senses start to kick in, and without looking behind me, I realize I seem to have someone who is going my way, which is understandable, but the odds that they too are buying birthday cards, men's underwear, lip gloss, toothbrushes, and gum is becoming a little concerning.

Finally, this person comes up from behind and stands a little too close to me, so before I speed off, I do a slight spin to see if I'm imagining things, and there is a middle-aged man who literally gasps when he sees me.

"My gawd. I thought you were my wife."

He rushes off looking very concerned. I was right. I was being stalked, but not in a bad way. He's the type of shopper who obviously lets his wife

143

do everything and he walks behind her for moral support, I guess, like a five-year-old.

I'm having a great chuckle behind my mask and then a few moments later I spy the happy couple. No wonder he thought I was his wife. We're the same height and weight, have the same unruly greyish hair, wear glasses, the same black mask, the same black coat, and the same black purse. Both of us dowdy, but with friendly eyes.

This story would be better if she'd been a real looker.

FOREST KINDERGARTEN

"I"

I WATCHED A DOCUMENTARY ABOUT A MOVEMENT IN DENMARK THAT TAKES THEIR preschoolers outside and lets them discover for themselves what the world has to offer. These little kids spend hours in the cold of winter, or in the spring mud, and their teachers let them crawl over big rocks, climb trees, and rough-and-tumble down hills. They use grown-up tools like hammers, saws, and nails, and learn to make fires, all while their teachers point out wildlife, insects, and foliage.

They learn by doing, touching, exploring, running, and falling. They are essentially allowed to "run with scissors." In the warmer months, they are barefoot; in the colder months, no one is chasing after them demanding they put on their hats and mitts. If their hands are cold, they'll put their mitts on eventually. It's up to them.

All the kids in this video had the rosiest cheeks, had snot running down their noses, and were covered with mud and slush. Their hair was matted and sticking up every which way. And as they ate their food by the fire, they looked incredibly happy.

The reporter stood open-mouthed as she watched one little fellow climb up to the top of a very tall tree.

"Don't you worry he'll fall off?" she asked one of the teachers.

"No," he answered. "They usually don't. We've only had one accident in all the years I've been doing this, and it was a parent who ran over a kid's foot with her car."

They showed the group of kids next to a babbling brook. They were allowed to run through it, but the kids themselves told the reporter that they weren't allowed to go near the deeper part without an adult. They were policing it themselves. The teachers trusted them not to go near it.

Now, the panicky mom in me felt my heart skip a beat at that particular scene, so would I be brave enough to let my little one run wild in the forest every day? As long as I wasn't there, I probably would, which will make my kids laugh if they read this, since I was such a worry-wart mother when my kids were little.

But I'm starting to change my mind, because as far as I can see, kids don't spend nearly enough time outside these days, and how do you learn to love the planet if you never see it, or spend time in nature? We all know how much better we feel when we've been out in the sunshine all day, with the wind in our hair and the smell of the earth all around us.

People my age (ancient) remember spending all day outside. We actually cherish those memories now. And we learned how to play with others, because back then, no mom or dad came running out of the house to rescue you. Kids picked on you and you cried, or you threw a punch and got punched back, and it didn't kill you. You learned who to stay away from and who you could depend on. And more importantly, you learned to rely on yourself, and kids don't get to do that much anymore. Not with helicopter parents constantly hovering overhead in case someone is mean to their baby. Kids really do need to get into altercations with kids their own age, so they can learn how to handle themselves in stressful situations. And to know that they don't always win.

Oh boy, I really do sound like an old fogey. When did that happen?

But it was the look on the kids' faces that stayed with me. They were having so much fun. And research suggests that playing with risk is vastly important to a human child's development. Play is important, period.

We should make sure that our kids enjoy the magic of the earth while they are living in the magic of their childhoods. A few bruises and scrapes while running with a stick is a small price to pay for the joy of pretending to be Robin Hood in Sherwood Forest.

FOOD FIGHT

"/,"

'M WRITING THIS IN JULY, SO THERE ARE SUMMER REFERENCES, BUT THIS SCENARIO describes any family get-together at any time of the year. The dilemma is always about trying to feed an extended group of people who are travelling great distances, and who will crash into each other head-on, in my case at the bungalow, for one long weekend.

Hubby and I are in the eye of the storm, since we live five minutes from the bungalow, so we are the ones who will be on duty when the troops arrive. And naturally people are dribbling in at very odd hours, because of work, or the distance they have to drive. There will be a car with a toddler in it, so who knows when they'll show up. Toddlers have their own schedule. There will be another car with two dogs in it, and we all know how that can go.

Add to the fact that some people are staying at our house, so now I have two fridges I need to fill. And I must point out that no one asked me to fill them. They do not expect anything. But I have turned into my mother at this point, and I really don't want the few days my sister gets to be here from Ottawa to be spent at Sobeys, so I'd like to prepare ahead of time, because that's what my anxiety brain is telling me to do.

And this anxiety brain is hubby's mortal enemy.

"*Relax*! It's just food. We'll figure it out."

"Spoken like a true man."

"Hey, I make my own meals, so don't insinuate that I don't do anything in the food department."

He's right about that. He shops, he cooks, he does dishes. And he has endless suggestions about what I should do.

147

"Just make a big pot of spaghetti and meatballs."

"And have the bungalow turn into a blast furnace before they get here?"

"Cook it at home."

"You can't eat spaghetti in the summer. It's just wrong. Besides, they said they probably won't be here for supper, and the kids aren't coming in until ten at night."

"So, there's Friday night taken care of."

"But I should make pizza. Everyone loves my pizza, and the kids expect it, and it would be good for lunch too, but I won't have enough."

"So, double the recipe."

Making eight pizzas is not for the faint of heart. Still. Now that it's in my brain, it has to be done.

"Should I make casseroles too?"

"Nah, I'll barbeque."

"How are you going to barbeque twelve steaks at one time?"

"Hamburgers and hot dogs it is."

"That's sort of boring."

"Lez...listen to me. Nobody's going to care."

"Or we could barbeque chicken. Or fat sausages. Well, I'm going to have to make potato salad and pasta salad and salad salad..."

"Take a breath. You don't have to do anything. Open a bag of chips and dip."

"John! How often does my family get together? I can't just throw a bag of Cheezies at them and yell, 'Dinner's served.'"

"I'd be happy."

"What do toddlers eat? I should have something for the little guy, but I have no idea what the rules are now."

"I'm sure his mother will take care of it."

I grab a pen and paper. "We have to make a list. I'm going to need shaved ham, shaved turkey, shaved chicken, sliced Swiss cheese, marble cheese, old cheese, Havarti, Kaiser rolls, mayo, mustard, tomatoes, lettuce, pickles, cucumber..."

"Take a breath."

"Oh, good gravy, I forgot about dessert!"

We never have dessert, because John is nuts and I'm on Weight Watchers.

"Do you know how hard it's going to be to make squares or cookies and not eat them? They're at least 25 points each."

"You don't have to."

"I don't?"

"Get some strawberries and Cool Whip."

Why didn't I think of that?

"I'll make the list for the beverages," hubby says.

I'm grateful. That's one less thing I have to think about. Then he ruins it.

"So, what does everyone drink?"

FEEDBACK

"|"

ONE OF THE GREATEST PLEASURES I GET FROM WRITING A COLUMN IS READING THE email I receive from people who view my weekly rantings.

And what's amazing is how many men write to me. Never expected that. But there are a whole lot of gentleman out there who feel the need to stick up for hubby. They know I'm only joking about him, but they feel a kinship with him and want me to know it. It's adorable, and John does get a kick out of it.

Certain columns get more of a response than others, and I always take note of it, just for my own sake. Knowing about the human condition helps me write my books. What are people really interested in? What hits them where it hurts? What are the struggles that affect all of us? I might be alone in my study, but I have a whole army of people who let me know that they, too, are suffering or rejoicing or dying of boredom.

Like my column about shopping with hubby to buy slippers, and the nonsense he put me though so he could buy a cheaper pair. My inbox was filled with women who know this particular struggle. One of them wrote, "What time shall I pick up my husband, because he's obviously at your house!"

Then there was the time I was approached in a women's washroom by a lady who tapped me on the shoulder. "Men!" she sniffed. "They drive you crazy. I'm glad to know I'm not the only one out here dealing with a cheapskate."

For the record, hubby is not a cheapskate with anyone else, just himself. Which drives me nuts. He'll spend a fortune on me or the kids but balks at twenty-dollar undershirts. You know, the nice ones that are soft and thick, something he should be wearing on cold winter days. But no, packs of three are good enough for him. Ugh.

There was a lot of response to a column I wrote about the perils of family visits, which are supposed to be a good time but often aren't. We had the terrible episode of our daughter's furry baby eating barbeque gunk the minute after she arrived from Halifax, and how the poor dog vomited in the house all weekend, which meant dealing with a distraught adult child who cast accusing glances at her father for not disposing of the mess properly.

"How did I know the foolish dog would find it?"

A woman wrote to me about the time her daughter arrived at the old homestead with her city dog in tow, and how the dog jumped out of the car and immediately took off like a shot after the free-range chickens in the yard, whereupon the frantic birds ran willy-nilly into the woods. The dad yelled at the daughter to control her dog and she shouted back that he was just a puppy and he didn't understand, and why weren't the stupid chickens in a coop! (I don't know the exact exchange, but we can all imagine what was said.)

Apparently, the chickens only returned to the yard under the cover of moonlight. I can see them now, tiptoeing quietly back to bed so as not to waken the hound.

One lovely lady from the Valley wrote to say she and her elderly brother live together and every Wednesday morning they read my column over breakfast at the kitchen table. That makes me so happy! The fact that people still eat breakfast together in the kitchen while reading the paper. It brings back memories of my father and grandfather. They too read the paper before heading out the door in the morning.

My column about the joy of receiving an actual letter in the mail in this day and age hit a nerve. Among the many emails about the subject, I received handwritten letters in my mailbox agreeing that it's a lost art. It was touching.

When I attended the Read by the Sea Summer Literary Festival in River John a couple of years ago and was signing books after a reading, a man came up to me and took a clipping out of his wallet. It was my column on birds, comparing different species with human-like traits.

"I loved what you said about crows sitting together in the backyard waiting to be fed. They do look like teenage boys hunched over smoking in the schoolyard. Thank you for that."

No, thank you. Thank all of you.

I'M BEAUTIFUL

"I"

I'VE BECOME ALLERGIC TO LOOKING AT MYSELF ON THE COMPUTER, THANKS TO ZOOM, Skype, and video messages being passed back and forth between us and the kids.

I watched a live video this morning of my baby blueberry crawling forward on her elbows, drooling and sucking on her lower lip as tooth number two makes its way into the world.

That's what I should've been concentrating on, but instead, because my computer is in front of a window, I was watching how the morning sun magnified my droopy eyelids, age spots, and wispy grey hair in technicolor.

Just when you think you don't look half-bad on a particular day, the computer dings and you swipe right and there's your family staring at you, and there you are, staring at yourself in the corner, looking like a wet teabag.

It does nothing for your self-esteem, but why worry? My style and fashion sense have been "who gives a shit?" for five months now. (Who am I kidding? It's been decades.)

But I cheered up immensely when I found a "housedress" with a zipper and big pockets yesterday at Walmart. Just like the ones my grandmother used to wear to clean our house in the morning, before she'd have her bath, get dressed, watch *The Edge of Night* and *Another World*, and then cook us dinner. (She wasn't a slave. She lived with us and this was her idea of a good time.)

This muumuu is the perfect solution for what to wear around the house during these days of COVID. No waistband. No bra. Big pockets for hiding handfuls of candy in a hurry. I believe my grandmother's generation called them "dusters."

And they remind me of all the fantastic Jewish moms in NDG, in Montreal, in the sixties, wearing loudly coloured housedresses, leaning over balconies with their cigarettes, gossiping with the next-door neighbours, and yelling at everyone's kids if the need arose.

I loved this and miss it desperately. Truly, I'm heartily sick of seeing women falling out of push-up bras with g-strung asses spilling everywhere, pouty lips and caked-on make-up, with black eyebrows so thick, they look alive.

On second thought, I rather like my lived-in face. It tells the world I've been here awhile, and I know a thing or two. Baby blueberry's face lights up when she sees it. That's all I ever need.

A SHOPPING TALE

"I"

I'M SURE WOMEN MUCH YOUNGER THAN I AM KNOW ALL ABOUT THIS PHENOMENON, BUT I'm new to the party. It's the latest marketing strategy of bombarding you with sales announcements via the internet.

Unaware of what I was getting myself into when the salesgirl asked for my email address, I gave it to her. "So, you'll know when the latest sales are on. It's very handy."

It sounded innocent enough, but it came to the point where there was a sales announcement every second day, all of them declaring it was the sale of the century and if you didn't act now you might live to regret it.

And although I knew that was nonsense, there was a little voice in the back of my head whispering, "Maybe they're right. Maybe I'll save a lot of money."

My mistake was telling hubby.

"If you just delete the email, you'll save a ton of money by not going near the joint."

It's easy to ignore logic like that.

Then I got a message saying that because I was their "bestest" customer ever, I was entitled to 40 percent off everything! And on top of that, because it was my birthday in June, I could get twenty-five dollars off anything I wanted. Well, gee whiz. That was pretty great.

So, I walked in the door and the place was crawling with women, all of them holding their cellphones and showing the sales ladies that they had been exclusively invited to the store because they were the bestest customer ever.

After finding a pair of pants that actually fit, I walked to the register. There was a quite a line of ladies in front of it. Goodness.

I joined the queue. And waited.

We waited so long, we eventually formed our own support group. It started with a few sheepish grins, and some eye-rolling and the grimaces you give each other when you realize you're all in the same boat, but eventually, I stood on one leg and then the other, putting my hand on my hip the way my mother used to when she was annoyed with me, and then I began to rubberneck towards the front cash to see what on earth was going on and why the line wasn't moving.

Turning to the woman behind me, I told her I was going to have to shoot myself. She told me to save a bullet for her.

And believe it or not, this backlog was caused by one woman. She kept one of the salesladies completely monopolized with endless requests and complaints, while the saleslady's hapless cohort tried desperately to deal with the rest of us.

This woman should be on a Wanted Poster in every retail establishment in the city. I have never heard such a litany of nonsensical excuses she came up with to try and shave extra money off every item in her cart. At one point she even went out to her car for something! Who does that?! Just when we thought she was finally done, it turned out she had stuff for her mother she needed to ring through. And then she wasn't even taking it with her, she wanted it all delivered and demanded the girl find out when that would be, so the saleslady had to make a phone call.

And not a backward glance at the increasingly desperate mob behind her. It takes a special kind of person to completely ignore everyone else.

When I finally made it to the salesgirl, I mentioned the twenty-five dollars off for my birthday. "Oh, that can't be combined with the sale. It has to be a regular ticketed item."

"Oh, well, I'll use it another time."

"It expires at the end of June."

Which was tomorrow, but I couldn't do it anymore. Not go back into the racks and look for anything else. Actual outdoor air was more important. I was in such a panic to leave, I didn't even wait for the poor girl to put my pants in a shopping bag.

"Don't you want a bag?" she called after me.

"No, thank you! I'm an old bag! I don't need another one!"

ANXIETY

"**/**"

A *NXIETY* IS A DULL WORD.
 I'd much rather say I have the collywobbles or jim-jams. That my heart is in my mouth, my stomach is in knots, I'm on tenterhooks, twitchy, in a stew, all a dither, in a tizzy, having kittens, het up, like a cat on hot bricks, squirrelly, or in a twit.

Look it up. These are just a few of the phrases or words associated with this phenomenon, which seems to indicate that we humans know this condition intimately. And quite frankly, at this time in our history, it's impossible not to be in a lather. But some of us are better at managing this distress than others.

As for me, I'm in the deep end of this particular pool. Always have been, but didn't know it. And now that this has been explained to me by professionals, my life suddenly makes sense.

So, I am on a path to try and manage my anxiety, which is giving me heart palpitations, something I'm trying to avoid.

I'm walking. Trudging, really. Out on cold, wet, and snowy mornings, slipping on ice, listening for cars, gripping my fingers inside my mittens to keep them warm. Isn't this wonderful? This is helping my frantic mind a lot. Now I have loads of time to think up catastrophic events as I move one foot in front of the other. But the experts say this is important, so I march on. Like a penguin.

Yoga. Another fabulous way to relieve stress. The trouble is I worry about what my bum looks like in yoga pants. I'm not sure I can bend in a way that will let me get back up. So, I've put that on hold, and it's eating away at me that I'm not making an appointment with a yoga facility.

Speaking of eating, I'm maintaining my commitment to no meat. I've eaten a case of chickpeas and lentils since January 1, and only had one minor incident. Hubby caught me.

"Why are there three pieces of bacon in the frying pan?"

"What bacon?"

"In the frying pan."

"That's for the cat."

"No, it's not."

"I swear. He asked me and I said he could have it."

"If you want bacon, Lesley, eat it. Just don't blame it on an innocent cat."

The guilt that comes with eating Wilbur is enormous.

Someone suggested I practice deep breathing for fifteen minutes, twice a day. This doesn't seem too hard, until you do it. You have to breathe in through your nose from your diaphragm, hold it as long as you can, and then breath out through your mouth slowly, taking your time between breathes.

Turns out I'm a lousy breather. And fifteen minutes is an incredibly long time.

I'm in my study on my chair with my eyes closed, trying to do this. The cat decides I require company, so he jumps from my desk and lands in my lap, which results in a quick expulsion of air I hadn't planned on.

Hubby's voice is droning on about something in the kitchen.

"I'm trying to relax!" I shout between breaths. "This is supposed to be calming, but how can I be calm when you're talking to me while I breathe?!"

He yells back. "Are you saying not to talk to you while you're breathing?"

"YES!"

"I guess this is my final farewell."

After five minutes, I hyperventilate. This requires practice.

A hot soak in the tub with Epsom salts is supposed to do wonders for your nerves. But only if you have two bathrooms in the house.

KNOCK KNOCK.

"I'm in the tub!"

"Well, hurry up!"

The whole point of a leisurely bath is to not hurry up.

They say a hobby is a good way to relax your mind. My hobby is writing novels. That's not always so relaxing, especially when I have to kill off a character I really like.

Hubby finds me in my study, sobbing.
"What's wrong?"
"Henrietta's toast!"
"Who's Henrietta?"
"No one you know! But she was really nice and I've just killed her!"
"I'm sure she deserved it."

AWARD SHOWS

"!"

THIS IS THE TIME OF THE YEAR WHEN MOVIE ACTORS CONGRATULATE THEMSELVES over and over again for basically doing their jobs. Is there any other profession that has more than one annual awards night?

We have the Golden Globes, The SAG, People's Choice, Oscars, MTV Movie, National Film, Critics' Choice, British Academy Film, New York Film, Independent Spirit, Hollywood Film, Golden Raspberry, Genie, and Golden Rooster Awards...not counting Google's list of the thirty-five film awards I haven't listed here.

Believe me, I don't mind watching bits and pieces of an award show, mostly to see what the ladies are wearing, but after you've seen one, you've basically seen them all. How much money went into those outfits, shoes, jewelry, food, and décor, not to mention the swag these people take home? The very people who can afford to buy this outrageously priced booty get it for nothing. That's enough to make anyone grumpy.

So, I've decided we need an award show for the rest of us. The ordinary folks who will never walk a red carpet in Hollywood. And we don't want a red carpet. We'd only have to vacuum it.

We'll call it the Mere Mortal Awards.

Best Supporting Actor: The friend who carried your sorry ass out of the bar and into a taxi, after an evening of dignified wine tasting.

Best Actor: The child who comes home three hours after curfew and tells you that it's not his fault because his car broke down, his phone died, he got mugged, and his wallet was stolen. Not to mention his friends leaving him in an abandoned warehouse on the outskirts of town. We should be happy and grateful he's still alive, after crawling all the way home in the dark.

Best Costume Design: Your six-year-old daughter, who insists at the top of her lungs that she wants to wear leopard leotards, her glittery tutu, a Screaming Eagles hockey jersey, and her new red rubber boots to her first day of Grade One.

Best Editor: The mother who makes the mistake of asking to see her child's essay homework assignment.

Best Director: The poor, long-suffering volunteer who organizes the parking lot at the Legion during the annual county fair.

Best Make-up and Hairstyling: Who are we kidding? Every fourteen-year-old girl on the planet.

Best Original Sound Mixing: A suburban family on a Saturday morning, while the dishwasher runs, the bacon sizzles, the phone rings, the doorbell chimes, the kids fight, the dog barks, the cat screeches, and a poor slob steps on a Lego piece.

Best Documentary: Our hapless dad, who does his best to capture his vacationing family on video, all the while said members run in every direction the minute he points the camera.

Best Original Screenplay: An angst-ridden teenage daughter's diary. There is no better dramatic rendition of everyday life than what lies between those locked pages, forever hidden away from prying eyes and little brothers.

Best Song: When the beloved family dog howls along, as we sing "Happy Birthday" around the kitchen table.

Best Picture: The entire clan sitting around the dinner table at Christmas, the kids at a card table at the end, everyone with their glasses raised amid the plates of turkey, stuffing, and cranberry. All the dear faces we love so much, and who we wouldn't trade for any amount of Hollywood glitz and glamour.

WHAT'S CHANGED?

"**/**"

WHAT'S CHANGED SINCE 2020?
You still have to clean the toilet, but toilet paper is like gold.

You used to stare at people in Asia on television for wearing masks on an ordinary day and think, "What's up with that?" Now you stare at people who don't.

What's a restaurant?

When someone forgets and reaches out to shake your hand, you run away.

The thought of being in a crowd gives you the willies.

You never take an elevator anymore. If you can't manage stairs, you stay home.

You now have a great excuse not to invite miserable Aunt Harriet over. "So sorry. We're only allowed ten people at the house."

A mask covers a double chin. Yay.

The dog gets walked four hundred times a day.

You're on a first-name basis with the UPS driver.

You're not invited to weddings anymore. This makes you either very sad or very happy.

What are you going to do with all your Air Miles and Aeroplan points?

Bedtime is now 9:30 P.M. Or 9:30 A.M. if you've binge-watched *The Crown.*

"Where do your children work?" "One is in the basement and one is at the dining-room table."

You miss everybody. Even people you never really liked.
Little kids must think their grandparents are just big giant heads.
Zoom is the most used word in the English language.
That and "F**k, I forgot my mask."

BACK UP

"**I**"

ARE ALL MEN AFFLICTED WITH THIS RIDICULOUS TRAIT? THE NEED TO BACK INTO every parking space on the planet?

Why is this necessary? Why can't they just pull into a space with the front end of their car like normal people? Like women?

It happened again last night. We were going to yet another dratted hockey game when hubby spied a coveted space near Centre 200. It looked like it was the only one left, and the race was on to grab it from some other old guy who doesn't want to walk too far on ice.

We approached, and it would have been like slipping a hand into a glove to just turn the car to the right with ease, but no. He drove past the space, leading the car behind us to believe it was their lucky day, but then braked and started to back up. I know the guy was cursing, because that's what I'd be doing, and now the car trying to get by us from the other side has to wait while the front end of our car nearly hits their front bumper and the two people walking into Tim Horton's suddenly have to give us a wide berth because of this three-point turn. There are now six people involved in this moment in time, when it could have been avoided by just moving forward between the lines.

"Was that necessary?"

Hubby didn't answer me. He never does. He's still dealing with this new car's backup camera, which is now covered with dirty snow crap.

"Which line am I supposed to go up to? Am I too close to the car behind me? Can you see?"

"No, I can't see, because I can't turn around in this seat with my seat belt on. If you'd just driven in, you'd be able to tell if you were too close because it would be in front of your face."

That's when he does stop and look at me. "If I remember correctly, it was you who wanted to have this backup camera in the car."

"I wanted it for when I'm backing up, not this nonsense. I've never backed into a parking space in my life, and I'm not going to start now."

Am I not correct? Isn't it just simpler to do it the right way? What is the advantage? So men can leave the parking space a whole two seconds earlier?

I'm pretty sure parking lots were designed for cars to drive into the space frontwards, because we're not dealing with a lot of room between the lines. Architects no doubt envisioned vehicles purring into slots one after the other with ease, not dealing with silly men who are turning themselves inside out, going around in circles, to stick their trucks' big rear ends in first.

Since there is no sensible explanation, I'm going to blame Dinky toys.

When little boys play with tiny cars on the floor, what do they do? They push them around, making zoom-zoom noises, and inevitably back them up into snug spaces before smashing them around in pretend car crashes and other catastrophes.

Guys just like that sort of stuff. The hairier the situation the better. They love getting trucks out of mud with chains and things, for some odd reason. So maybe this situation isn't entirely their fault. It's in their DNA, perhaps.

And to be fair, I confess to having my own bad habit when dealing with driving. I won't turn left at a stop sign and cross four lanes of traffic, even if I have to go that way. I'll turn right and find the nearest side street, pull into someone's driveway, and turn around. Most women I know do too.

So, I'm going to put down this behaviour as an innate compulsion. Men just can't help themselves, so I might as well save my breath and let it go.

Hubby will be very glad to hear it.

P.S. I discussed this with two of my besties recently and was horrified to learn that they back into parking spaces too, so apparently I'm very wrong in thinking this is a male problem. Harrumph.

P.P.S. This column generated the most feedback I've ever had. Hundreds of men telling me I was an idiot. Even my auto-insurance guy weighed in.

SHOULDA, WOULDA, COULDA

"**I**"

GUILT IS A FOUR-LETTER WORD IN MY BOOKS.

It's the one thing that drives me mad about myself. My guilt about everything. It's a terrible affliction that only I can control, but it doesn't seem to matter. The minute I stop feeling guilty about one thing, another one pops up to fill the void. Apparently, I once ordered two tons of guilt to fall on my shoulders every January for the rest of my life, and I have since lost the order form to cancel it.

Telling people to stop feeling guilty is like telling them to stop drowning this instant. It doesn't work unless you have a life jacket, a cute lifeguard, a buoy, and a boat handy. And I have none of those things.

Everyone feels guilty about something. And those who don't, feel guilty about it. They know they should, so what's wrong? Are they not sensitive enough? Are they cold fish? Are they sociopaths?

The only thing that gives me comfort is knowing that most humans running around this earth are busy with this mental condition as well. But how did we get this way? What comfort do we derive in ruminating about not spending enough time with our kids, or our parents, or our grandparents, or our friends or our pets? The only thing it does is make us feel lousy about ourselves.

And then a talking head comes on television to tell us we should be

167

taking care of ourselves first. If we don't look after ourselves, how are we going to look after anyone else? So, there's something else to fret about. I'm not just ignoring my posse, I'm ignoring moi.

Should I be going to yoga retreats, or meditation retreats, or spa retreats, or retreat retreats? Even if I could afford to, should I spend that money on myself when the kids could always use some, or hubby needs a new lawn mower, or another charity needs it, or one more crowdfunding message pops up?

When should we stop feeding the birds? They are outside now, looking forlornly at the feeders. How can you ignore a bawling fat cat, even when you know he's fat? How do you say no to a cashier who asks you to donate to the children's hospital, or the Salvation Army, even though you've given donations five times this week?

It's impossible not to feel like a heel if you don't have a hot meal on the table when the troops come in the door. Or if your kids have more than one hole in their socks. Or if you can't make a baseball practice, because you're on a stretcher in the emergency room.

It's always the same when my sister or hubby's brother call us from Ontario. "When are you two coming up this way?"

"Hopefully this year. How are the grandchildren? They must be three by now."

"Adrien is going into junior high, Chloe is off to space camp this summer, and the baby starts kindergarten in the fall."

"You're joking! How's Snoopy?"

"Snoopy's been dead for five years. You haven't met Sherman, our now middle-aged bull mastiff."

Just wonderful. Now I'm mad at everyone for putting so much pressure on me. I can't be everywhere at once, since I have important things to do, and important places to go. Not that I can think of any at the moment, but still.

The guilt that's bothering me the most lately is trying to decide what to do with my mother's glassware. She left me an entire credenza filled with cornflower blue glasses. Glasses that are too small to be meaningful in today's mega, gallon-sized world. And I know for a fact that my kids don't want them. The glasses stare at me when I'm watching television. "Don't you dare throw us out! What would your mother say?"

The fact that I can't remember my mother ever using these glasses, except for maybe at Christmas dinner, doesn't make a difference. Giving them away would be like throwing my mother out the door in a blue box on recycle day and watching her call for help from the curb.

It's not really different with our parents' old photo albums. While I could never, ever, throw any of them out, it means my kids will be stuck with twenty boxes of pictures, most of them of people they've never met.

Isn't it funny that I don't feel guilty about that? It's payback for all their junk I still have cluttering up my house, because they don't want it cluttering up their houses.

CROSSWORD PUZZLES

"I"

A S IF I DON'T HAVE ENOUGH TO DO WITH WORDS IN MY WORK LIFE, I'VE SUDDENLY become obsessed with crossword puzzles. I've turned into an old woman drinking coffee with the paper folded and a pen in hand, which drives hubby nuts.

"Why can't you use a pencil, like the rest of the world?"

"I can't see it when it's in pencil."

"You can't read it when it's in pen and you've scratched out all the letters ten times."

"It's my puzzle. Keep your nose out of it."

If I get a word wrong, I don't care, and I don't necessarily finish them either. If I've been back to the same clue more than necessary, I'll ignore it. Not for me, looking it up on Google or grabbing the thesaurus. I'll fill anything in, just to make it look finished. The key is to not stress over it. It's supposed to be mindless, and at the same time, keep your brain ticking over so we don't molder away into that good night.

My problem is admitting I don't know everything, but sometimes I have to, like when I'm in my lounge chair in the living room and John is in the kitchen, dirtying every dish we own just to heat up a can of soup for lunch.

"What was the father's name on the Cartwrights' television show?"

"You never watched *Bonanza*?"

"No."

"How is that possible?"

"I didn't have brothers and I don't like cowboys. Just answer the question."

"Pa."

"His name was Pa?"

"Yep."

"It's three letters."

"Ben."

"B-E-N. Thanks."

"I can't believe you never watched *Bonanza*."

"Drop it! What's the name of the Minnesota football team?"

"Is this a joke?"

"I don't watch football. What's their name?"

"The Vikings."

"What a stupid name. What has Minnesota got to do with Vikings?"

"What does Pittsburgh have to do with Pirates? It's just a name."

Crossword puzzles can lead to heated arguments if you're not careful.

The clues I hate are suffixes. That smacks of grammar, and I hate grammar. Hard to believe that I'm a writer. I only go by sound. If something sounds right, it's right. That doesn't always work, but I'm too afraid of grammar to care. Editors come in very handy.

There is a pleasure surge that bubbles up when you look at a blank crossword puzzle and instantly realize you know all the words in the top left block. Does everyone start there or is it just me?

But there is total gloom when my eye falls on a four-letter word for a Celtic letter, or a four-letter word for Spanish hors d'oeuvre, or a five-letter Latin verb. What's a sombrero go-with, or who is Soprano __ Gluck? A Spanish pronoun or NATO cousin isn't fair.

However, the more I do, the more I realize there are perennial favourites with crossword puzzle makers. Now I know that a brownish tint is ecru, and the language of Pakistan is Erdu, but I haven't figured out what Kashmir cash is, or Cantina toast.

Hubby does the *New York Times* crossword puzzle. And he keeps at it until it's done. It could be weeks. I'd rather poke my eyeballs out than go over and over the same clues day after day, but I do find, if I walk away from a puzzle and go back the next day, I almost immediately get the rest of the clues. A good night's sleep does help.

What doesn't help is having someone come and fill in a few clues for you when you aren't looking.

"Hey! Did you do this?" I point at my newspaper.

"Do what?"

He's stalling, so I poke my finger into the newspaper several times. "This! It's almost finished!"

"I just did a few you couldn't get."

"It's not that I couldn't get them! It was midnight, so I went to bed. Do I have to put up a big sign saying DON'T TOUCH from now on?"

"You already have one. It's on your side of the bed."

DENTAL WOES

"I"

I'M NOT SURE I SHOULD ADMIT THIS, BUT MY FILE AT THE DENTIST'S OFFICE IS ENOR-
mous. They bring it in with a backhoe, because I am their prize patient. They could trot me out at conferences as the weird specimen who, over the course of a lifetime, has had every dental procedure known to mankind.

Truthfully, I've always been rather ashamed of this fact. How can it be that someone who has always taken care of their teeth is such a shoddy example of dental care? It's not like my mother put me to bed with a lollipop every night. I've always brushed and flossed faithfully, yet every time I go to the dentist, I have to have something done.

And not only done, but done several times. Ask my poor, harried dentist. She always shakes her head when she sees me coming.

"Oh lordy, what now?"

"I broke a tooth, broke my appliance, and have an achy area somewhere in the back of my mouth."

"And it's only Monday," she sighs.

By rights, I should hate dentists. Once, when I was seven or eight, I had a dentist whose first name was Leslie. His dental assistant's name was Leslie as well. When I walked in, he had a great laugh with the pretty assistant about the three Leslie/Lesleys in the room. He was so chuffed, he ended up drilling a hole through the side of my mouth. I distinctly remember him saying, as he wiped up the gushing blood, "No need to trouble your mother with this. It happens sometimes." So, I kept my sore mouth shut, as kids usually do when an adult tells them to.

I should've kicked him.

Then there was the dentist who offered my father free dental services for some publishing work. He happened to work in the same building as my dad. Dad thought this was a great idea. Trouble was, I realize now that this dentist never used freezing. He made his patients white-knuckle it through the appointment. Looking back on it, I should've not only kicked him but put him in a headlock. My dad didn't believe me, because he never had to have any work done.

"Don't be silly, child. Of course he uses freezing. He's not a torturer."

Uh, yeah. He was.

Finally, sixty-two years later, I found out the reason behind my horrible dental journey, after I went to a specialist this week for a root canal. I'm floored that I still have root canals that need doing, since every one of my molars has been mined for diamonds.

He took one look inside my mouth and said, "Where were you born?"

"Montreal."

"AH-HA!! I knew it!" he cried.

"Knew what?"

"You're exactly the right age. Mayor Jean Drapeau thought fluoride was a Communist plot, and refused to put it in the city's water."

"So, it's not my fault I have lousy teeth! I'm sending my dental bills to the estate of Jean Drapeau. The amount is in the millions by now."

Then I asked him about the Montreal dentist who never used freezing. He tells me there were quite a few dentists back in the day who didn't believe in it. And naturally, just my luck, my dad worked next to one.

I remember being so proud when my kids had their dental checkups and were told they had no cavities. It's like I was personally responsible for this achievement. Unfortunately, it's not something you can bring up at a dinner party.

"Our Harvey has won a scholarship to Yale."

"Well, our Priscilla is going to the Olympics."

"Oh yeah? I'll have you know that my kids have no cavities. So there. Put that in your pipe and smoke it."

If there's anyone out there who was born in Montreal in the fifties and sixties, know that your rotten teeth are thanks to the guy who brought us Expo 67.

THE REMOTE

"I"

WATCHING TELEVISION USED TO BE A PLEASURABLE EXPERIENCE. WE HAD FOUR channels and turned a knob to change them. The knob was on the television, so you always knew where to find it. There was no fighting over what to watch. You could take it or leave it. Saturday night was *Hockey Night in Canada*. If you didn't like hockey, you were out of luck. You played with paper dolls or read your sister's diary.

I'm so old I remember when the television blared "O Canada" before turning to static at midnight. That was your signal to go to bed. I used to curse when I was up nursing my infant and the television went dead. Watching some horrible detective show was better than sitting in the dark waiting for baby to fall back to sleep. At least it drowned out my husband's snoring.

Today there are so many ways to watch television I can't keep up with it. We have too many remotes in this house and I have no idea how to use them. I've figured out the main one, to a point. But if, God forbid, I press the wrong button, that's the next forty minutes of my life gone, while I press every other button trying to make something work. Then I have to holler to hubby, who always rolls his eyes and tells me he's already told me how it works a hundred times and why don't I ever listen?

"What will you do when I die?!" he frets.

Never watch television again?

Then we got Netflix and I had to haul the computer out near the television to plug wires into it.

"What wire goes where? How do you hook up the sound? What channel is this supposed to be on?"

Have you ever looked at the back of a television set now? Do you know how many wires are coming out of that thing? It's a nightmare if you accidentally drop one wire and can't figure out where it goes. It's a good twenty minutes of hollering at each other before we eventually get it right. By then the popcorn is cold, the pop is flat, and you don't want to be in the same room as your mate.

So, our kids try and make things easier with a Comcast device. HAH! It works sometimes but not always. I spend twenty minutes running from room to room, trying to click the right buttons and make sure movies are loading, but then they don't, or they freeze, or they start loading again. Time to call my kids, who sigh over the phone and walk me through it, but that never helps.

"Don't know what to tell you, Mom. It should work."

"Well, it doesn't."

"Where's the box? There should be instructions."

"Not sure."

"You're supposed to keep stuff like that."

"Oh, baloney. You sound like your father."

But the worst thing is going to visit your kids. They have the latest in television technology, which means that not only can they watch shows, they are now hooked up to their Xboxes or PlayStations, and their remote looks like something out of *Star Trek*. I tried to press a button to turn on the television the last time I was there and it said, "Hi, Paul."

Do you think I could figure out how to watch the *Marilyn Dennis Show*? There were three thousand channels to pick from and I haven't found it yet.

Now I know why people binge-watch their programs. Once you finally have your show on, you don't dare turn anything off, in case you can't find it again.

SELF-HELP

"**!**"

'M THE FIRST TO ADMIT THAT I HAVE TRIED A LOT OF THERAPY AND OTHER KINDS OF
self-help and self-improvement in my lifetime. My latest venture comes
in the form of these columns, where I blather on about things that annoy
me and people read it. Obviously, I have no shame, and I hope people recognize themselves in these weekly hissy-fits and feel better knowing there
is someone out there who is more pathetic than they are.

I'm at your service.

Everything we read advises us to seek help when we need it, and therapy comes in many forms. There is something for everyone. While I have
failed at all of them, the bright spot is that I'm obviously not a quitter.

Someone once gave me a positive-affirmation tape. It had melodious
background music, and on one side you could hear the affirmations out loud
and on the other side it was subliminal. I was to repeat the affirmations as
if I already believed them.

"I am calm, confident, and self-assured." Umm...no.

"I believe in myself." Not really.

"I am filled with self-love." HA!

Realistically, I should've known it wouldn't work, because the doctor
on the tape said to sit in a quiet spot and listen to it ten times a day. It was
thirty minutes long. When would I pick up the kids after school or take them
to ballet and hockey, and make sure supper was on the table?

Then I got a tape of self-guided mediations. Get in a safe place and close
your eyes. I can't tell you what the voice said next, because I was asleep in

a matter of seconds. So, I tried to just sit cross-legged and mediate with my eyes open, focusing on one spot in the room. Quickly I became focused on how my knees were killing me.

They say to ignore your thoughts. Just let them go and mind your breathing, so now I'm fighting with my thoughts inside my own head, but it's not going well.

When I first tried acupuncture, I pictured myself on my back, relaxing on a bed having it done. No. You have to sit on a table hunched over trying to hide your belly rolls as they stick needles in the back of your neck, your feet, and your cheeks.

A naturopath gave me a sheet of paper that contained my new diet. No bread, no pasta, no meat, no dairy, no alcohol. As you can imagine, I lasted until sundown that same day.

It's best to forget the yoga incident.

Swimming proved a problem when I forgot my water shoes and imagined foot fungus all over the damp tiles. There was no private change room, and I had to undress behind a skimpy towel. My new highlights got wet and water went up my nose. Then I walked out to the car with my wet hair in minus-thirty weather.

Lifting weights was promising, but I was cautious and started with just three pounds. I developed tendinitis in both wrists.

Then there was the appointment with an osteopath. It's like getting a massage from a grizzly bear. It reminds you that you have a body, because absolutely all of it hurts.

A girlfriend asked me to go to a painting-and-wine party. They provide the supplies and you just paint what they tell you to and sip wine. Since I don't drink (which is a therapy I really should try), I brought a can of Diet Pepsi. The woman wanted us to paint a fence, a beach, the water, the sky, and a pair of flip-flops. I asked if I could paint a cat.

"F**K NO" was her answer. Honest to God. So, I made sure I painted a cute little green worm with a big smile on his face in the bottom right corner of my canvas, just to bug her.

My favourite therapy at the moment is going to the movies by myself every Tuesday afternoon. For two hours, I'm not driving myself crazy with my innermost thoughts.

[Author's note: The movie thing stopped in March 2020.]

DRY EYES

"**!**"

YOU KNOW HOW YOU LIVE YOUR LIFE DAY-TO-DAY, AND MOST OF THE TIME YOU'RE okay, despite the usual aches and pains that come with being as old as dirt; and then one day out of the blue you realize you're not okay, or at least there's something bugging you, and it's taken about six months for you to realize it? But once you're aware of it, that's all you can think about.

This happened to me recently. For months I thought I was either suddenly allergic to our cat or we were having a pollen explosion in the middle of winter. My eyes, which I've never given a thought to my entire life, were suddenly front and centre in the "this is really bugging me" department.

They were always sore, or itchy, or burning, or scratchy, or felt very, very tired. I was constantly rubbing them, which is not a good thing when you occasionally wear mascara. The day I discovered this, I was in Pennington's shopping for a pair of pants and looked in the mirror while I was in the dressing room. A grumpy-looking raccoon stared back at me.

Even hubby noticed after a while. "You're constantly rubbing your eyes. Is there a reason?"

"The better to see you with, my dear."

Later that night, as I sat and watched *Grey's Anatomy*, a commercial came on with Serena Williams jumping around a tennis court before she sat down and put eye drops in her eyes, so I unmuted the commercial. "Do you suffer from dry eyes? Get relief now!"

Dry eyes. I'd heard of it but never gave it much attention. Maybe that's what I had. When the thought of pouring a gallon of lubricating eye drops in each eye becomes more desirable than eating a whole pizza, you know you have a problem. Time to call the eye doctor.

She checked me out.

"This happens to a lot of women as they get older. It's hormonal."

Of course it is. Hormones and females go together like mac and cheese. Just when I thought I was past the age of worrying about hormones. But apparently, they stick to you like glue to the grave.

"Are you in front of a computer all day?"

"Kind of. I write novels and weekly columns where I complain about everything under the sun, like my itchy, miserable eyes."

"You can turn down the brightness on your computer screen. It might help."

"Do they have a setting called gloomy?"

"Do you drink lots of water?"

Okay. This is like being asked how much you weigh. We always lie about it for some reason. We don't want to admit that we don't drink eight glasses of water a day like we're supposed to. It's like telling the principal that we skipped school.

"Umm, I brush my teeth twice a day. Does that count?"

It doesn't.

She tells me that studies show fish oil helps, but you have to be on it for more than six months before you potentially feel a difference. So, I'll add that huge plastic bottle to the fifty other huge plastic bottles hubby and I have lined up on the kitchen counter. No wonder we can never get out of the house before 9:00 A.M. It takes us an hour and a half every morning to down all our drugs. Hey! I forgot to tell her that I drink water to swallow my vitamins and calcium tablets, so that has to count.

A humidifier in the bedroom would help me, apparently. Just what I need. Another machine to drown out the noise from my CPAP machine. Our bedroom will soon be noisier than a construction site.

And lastly, I need a lifetime supply of eye drops, and they aren't cheap. Now I carry drops with me constantly. I'd make a necklace out of the little droppers if I could. And I have to put ointment in my eyes at night. Have you ever put what amounts to Vaseline in your eyes before you go to bed? It's alluring.

Between my smeary eyes, my face mask, and my dental retainer that keeps me from grinding down what's left of my teeth, I am simply a vision.

"John? John? Are you in here? Hello?!"

FAIL ARMY

"**/**"

I F YOU'VE EVER SEEN A FAIL ARMY VIDEO, YOU KNOW YOU'RE IN FOR: A LOT OF MEN
riding bikes too fast down steep cliffs, only to disappear as they face-plant
into a cloud of dust. Or more men who jump on railings with their skate-
boards, and then land on their crotches, fall off, and writhe with agony while
their pals laugh their heads off.

Then we have ladies attempting a yoga headstand only to fall into their
Christmas trees, or they swing around a pole in their bedrooms and go
flying into the bureau when the pole decides it has had enough of this kind
of treatment.

Very funny. But you don't have to go to those extremes to have something go wrong and cause uncontrollable hilarity.

Have you ever been in a dressing room, stuck in an outfit, with your
hands over your head, while your daughter is unaware and shopping somewhere else in the store? You frantically whisper her name through the
crack in the door, hoping she'll hear you and come to the rescue, but it's the
saleslady that hears your pleas for help. "Oh, that's okay," you say when she
asks if you need assistance. I do need someone to come to the rescue, but
only a family member or best friend can witness this disaster.

While staying with my daughter once, she showed me a new face mask
she bought, and said we should both try it. I was leery, because it was as black
as coal. She assured me it would peel right off after it dried. We frightened
the dog when we went downstairs to sit and wait it out. When the timer
went off, we both went into the bathroom and looked in the mirror while

we peeled off the mask. The trouble was, her mask did come off, but mine was sludgy goop. I had tar on my face and I couldn't remove it. Sarah was no help at all. She was too busy holding onto her ribs.

My grandmother once told me a story about her sister Muriel. They were grown women at the time, and they went berry picking. Muriel got caught short and had to use an old outhouse. She went in, and ten seconds later came flying out with her underpants around her ankles, hobbling through the field with a swarm of wasps behind her.

Now that sounds downright dangerous, but whenever they repeated that story, the two of them would burst out laughing. I got more of a kick out of them laughing than from the story itself.

Grammie's other sister, Betty, told us the story about a woman who owned a boarding house. She went upstairs with a load of fresh laundry and the door to the bathroom was open and steamy. Her husband, standing with his back to her, had one foot up on the side of the tub, drying himself off. She reached between his legs and pulled. "Ding-dong. Avon calling." Her boarder turned around and she was so mortified, she slipped on the bathroom floor in her bid to escape and broke her leg.

We always laughed at my poor father, who was the clumsiest man alive. When I was there visiting once I heard Dad downstairs with what sounded like an electric saw. "What's he doing?" I asked my mother.

She shrugged. "God knows."

The noise stopped, and we heard him trudging up the stairs. The door opened and he was completely white, with billowing clouds of Gyproc dust advancing up the basement stairs behind him. He took off his goggles and had two circles of white dust around his eyes. "Well, that was a mistake." Mom screamed and slammed the door in his face to prevent a dust emergency in the kitchen. Apparently, you can't use a power saw on Gyproc.

Another time he decided to seed the backyard. A howling windstorm blew into the neighbourhood, but he persisted. In the spring, the lawn looked like a giant cinnamon bun, with circular streaks of grass amongst the dirt.

When my sister first took her new French boyfriend sailing, she tacked into the wind and yelled, "Duck!" He stood up and looked around. "Where?"

The mast hit him in the chest and down he went.

They got married anyway.

FAILED ATTEMPTS

"!"

SOMETIMES I'M JUST TOO FOOLISH FOR MY OWN GOOD.
    I love my vegan cookbooks. Really. I've had a lot of success with the recipes, even though I'm the only one eating them in this house. Not that hubby doesn't want to be healthy too, it's just that his idea of healthy eating involves barbecued rib steaks. Try as I might, he's not that into marinated tofu cubes.

The other day I was making what some might call power bars. The kind of snack you can grab and put in your purse if you're on your way to an appointment and don't have time for lunch. There's lots of goodies in them, like pecans, dried cranberries, oats, rice cereal, almond butter, and seeds.

While I was putting the recipe book away, it happened to open to a page showing a very crispy cracker, the kind that nature-loving, Birkenstock-wearing hippies like myself would love to have in a glass container on a kitchen counter to impress guests.

It was a gorgeous cracker, smeared with guacamole, so I glanced up at my open pantry shelves where I squirrel away squirrel food in see-through jars, and lo and behold, I had everything I required! Chia seeds, raw hulled sunflower seeds, raw white sesame seeds, and raw pepitas seeds. All I needed to add to the recipe was water, garlic, and Herbamare (or seasoned salt for you hubby types).

Mix together and lay out flat on sheet and bake at 300 degrees for about an hour, turning halfway through the cooking process.

Oh, goodie. I'd have lovely, crisp crackers to dip into things like hummus, or just a thin, crunchy snack on its own. Who's the smartest girl alive? My internal organs were clapping with joy at my dedication to mindful clean eating. Not for me, a trip to the middle aisle of the grocery store to pick up fat-laden, calorie-busting, trans-fat-and-salt-infused factory crackers! NO!

I was a food saint.

I was worried.

The recipe mentioned to watch the crackers carefully because they could burn, so I peered into the oven at one-minute intervals. It's not a good idea for anxious people to hear things like that. Now I was personally responsible for the health and safety of these various seeds.

The crackers didn't really look like the crackers in the picture. They were sort of similar, but not really. What was I doing wrong? I did exactly what they told me too. Well, maybe if I just waited until they're done, they'd look a bit better.

After taking them out of the oven, unburned, I gave a huge sigh of relief. Now it said to let them cool on the sheet. Maybe they'd look different after they cooled.

They cooled for a couple of hours, just to be sure. Then I took one piece of cracker and turned it over before breaking it into pieces, like I was supposed to.

This wasn't the crisp cracker of my dreams. This looked like a sheet of carpet underlay. Sort of felt like it too.

Rats.

Now, I suppose I could put them back in the oven for three more hours, but who has that kind of time? There's only one thing to do. I don't break it so much as bend it into little pieces and take my failed crackers and offer them to the squirrels, crows, blue jays, mourning doves, and other little critters in the backyard.

Chalk it up to misfortune.

It was also unfortunate that while I was writing this column, I burnt the bottom of my favourite big pot when the water evaporated while boiling ears of corn. Now the rabbits are happy too.

Bottom line, don't write about cooking while you're cooking.

BTW...the birds refused to eat the crackers.

ARGUING

"**I**"

I CAN'T BELIEVE IT!

Just yesterday, I read a fascinating article on the internet. On a well-known site called 77 Recipes, so it must be legit. The headline read "PSYCHOLOGY SAYS COUPLES WHO ARGUE ACTUALLY LOVE EACH OTHER MORE."

"Many studies have shown that people who argue really love each other more. Psychologists believe that the main reason for it is the communication between those two people. They argue about every problem, and they solve it before it becomes too late. They have different opinions, but always found the best solution for their relationship. It is very important for couples to explain their needs clearly and try to adapt their selves to the other partner. If you and your partner argue a lot, it means that your relationship is successful and you should continue fighting about it."

Strangely, no one took credit for writing this article, but after reading it, I know why. The individual has a point, but also grammar and tense issues.

Hubby and I argue continuously over everything, and we've been married for forty-two years. We have a friend who is a minister, and she counsels soon-to-be-married couples. She said one couple came in and squabbled the entire hour. She said they'd be fine because they reminded her of hubby and me.

I've had more than one divorced friend confess that they never argued with their ex-husband. How is this possible? John and I argue over changing a light bulb. And what garbage bags to use. And how much cat food we should be doling out. And what flavour.

Granted, it's exhausting, but I never feel ignored.

Maybe that's where it comes from. We are both extremely nosy about what the other one is doing.

"I'm going to town."

"What for?"

"Stuff."

"Like what?"

"I don't know. Maybe some clothes or shoes or toothpaste."

"I need to cut down some trees."

"And why does that concern me?"

"You might want to be around in case I fall off the ladder."

"Oh, wonderful. I get so stay home because you might fall off a ladder."

"Well, I don't have to do it I guess."

"No, you don't. I'll be back in a couple of hours."

"The flies will be bad by then."

"So, you're saying you don't want me to go?"

"You can do what you like."

"So why bring up this nonsense about cutting trees?"

"I just thought you'd like to know."

But there are several ways you can argue. Most of the time we bicker, which is arguing over petty and trivial nonsense that doesn't matter one way or the other. We don't even notice it anymore, but I'm sure we drive everyone around us crazy. To bicker is on par with a scrap, or a spat, or a spar, or a wrangle. It's quite amazing how many words we have for this condition.

Then we have a more serious situation, when you quarrel or dispute or fight, or have words, lock horns, or, worse, are at each other's throats. This can get ugly, and if at all possible, you should avoid this situation. It takes up too much of your precious energy.

But then you have The Big One. Not speaking to each other. Is there anything worse that waking up and having to make coffee when one of you is at the sink and won't move? Instead of saying a cheery "Good morning" and politely nudging them out of the way with a peck on the cheek, you stand behind them with your hand on your hip and scowl, hoping your laser-beam eyes will drill a hole through their stubborn head. They pretend not to notice you and saunter away at their leisure. You resist the urge to throw a dishtowel at them.

If you do spend a day not talking to your spouse, it's alarming how small your house becomes, because they always seem to be in your face. This is the time to go to the movies by yourself, or have coffee with a girlfriend.

Fortunately it doesn't last long, and before you know it, you're back to talking about the cat or asking if the kids called while you were out. I think the key to a good marriage is knowing you can have an argument, but you are reassured that you're each other's best friend, so wait for a few minutes and your life will continue as it should.

BIRD BRAINS

"!"

TO CALL SOMEONE A BIRD BRAIN IS SUPPOSED TO BE AN INSULT. ALTHOUGH, HUMAN beings manage to insult everything. How this makes us the superior species, I have no idea. We have a very long way to go before we can count ourselves as intelligent as the animal kingdom.

Hummingbirds in particular make my heart happy. These tiny toddlers of the sky have huge personalities. We spend our summers at the bungalow watching this original reality show for hours on end through our windows, or sitting in the swing on the deck. This time of year is particularly frantic. Everyone is bulking up for the prolonged trip back across the Gulf of Mexico. Imagine that! From Homeville to South America! It makes my head spin. How is this possible?

By the end of the summer, I can almost tell our gang apart. We have one very plump male ruby-throat, who spends his every waking moment in the weigela bush by the cottage door, guarding his feeder. I call him Fat Bastard. I have yet to see another hummingbird try to take a sip out of his red diner. He is so fast; he can dive out of the sky and knock off two females with a single swoop. Sharing is not in his vocabulary. If he were a human named Fred, I'd hate him for being so mean-spirited, but there is something about his single-mindedness. I admire his tenacity.

"The girls," as I like to call them, have staked out their own territory. One sits in the apple tree, and she has a view of two sides of the cottage, and therefore can see all five feeders at once. One of this year's crop (you can tell because they are so fragile and slender) has taken up guard in the spruce tree above our swing. Another one likes to perch on the overhang of the roof.

You can be out on the swing in the morning enjoying a cup of coffee and suddenly four females will start a relay race, chattering and buzzing as they zip right past your head. One actually stopped in midair about three inches from my nose. My immediate notion was to reach out and kiss her, but she was gone before I finished the thought.

I love changing the feeders with fresh sugary water, because I keep the syrup in the fridge, and when they first taste the cold liquid they do a double-take and come back to drink in the cool loveliness. These are the times I've seen three or four on the same feeder, gulping happily as it becomes a merry-go-round.

It's so lonely when they gradually disappear, one by one. The males bugger off first. They leave the cleaning up to the ladies, surprise, surprise. And then you keep your eye on them to make sure one of them doesn't stay too long. There's always a fine line, between wanting them to get fuelled up for the return journey and fretting that the weather is getting cold and they need to go for their own sakes.

Maybe the fact that they are only here for the golden summer months makes us nostalgic for them throughout the year. Or the idea that they travel so incredibly far to share our summers with us. Their tiny hearts and wings, beating so impossibly fast, makes me think that miracles do exist.

BUBBLES

"I"

S O, HUBBY CAME INTO MY STUDY THE OTHER DAY AND SAID THAT WE WERE ALLOWED to "bubble" with one other family unit.

I didn't catch what he said after that, as I was too busy throwing the pyjamas I live in into a Sobeys bag, grabbing the car keys, and bolting out the door to drive to Halifax to see my baby granddaughter! She's almost five months old! I haven't seen her in three months. That's more than half her life!!

As I roared up the driveway, I did shout at John to say that I'd see him in about a year, but he disappeared in a cloud of dust, so who knows what he said after that.

Next, I called my daughter to tell her I loved her very much but not as much as I love this baby, so I'd wave to her as I zoomed by in the car when I got to the big city. She and her brother live on the same street, so it's a little awkward.

Because of my determination to keep my baby safe, my usual ten pee stops from Homeville to Halifax were reduced to one quick visit to a gas station in Antigonish. Exit 33, I believe. It's amazing what one steely grandmother can accomplish when she sets her mind to it. And at that stop, I was wearing a mask, gloves, snorkel, oxygen tank, garbage bags, saran wrap, tinfoil, and an umbrella to keep people at bay. Strangely, people seemed to avoid me, so I needn't have worried.

My baby (that's right, she doesn't belong to anyone else) told me she was waiting for me to come. That if I hadn't shown up soon, she was going to file a missing person report.

She and I are in cahoots already. We are a team. I will be here for her for the rest of her life.

Grandad will be here next week, because he's a normal person.

MUSICAL CHAIRS

"I"

W HERE WE SIT CONCERNS US GREATLY.
Have you noticed that if you invite someone for dinner and they happen to sit in *your* chair before you can direct them to another one, you get all out of gear? And everyone else at the table keeps looking at you, knowing that this arrangement feels awkward. The poor guest is thankfully unaware of the tragedy, unless you flat out can't stand it and say, "Umm...that's my chair." Obviously, this would only happen with someone you know well, and not your husband's boss.

It's the same thing when your adult kids come home. One of them sits in your chair in the living room. That's just not right. The television is turned perfectly for viewing at your angle. Now you're relegated to the hapless loveseat in the corner because, let's face it, it would be churlish to kick them out of it after they drove five hours to come and see you. However, it doesn't stop you from fidgeting relentlessly to find a comfortable spot on the stupid loveseat.

The movie theatre is a hotbed of emotion when it comes to picking a chair. Hubby, as everyone must know by now, only likes to sit in the very back row of a theatre, so no one can cough or sneeze on him. He also likes the middle, which is why he's always three hours early for a show. Now, if by some chance there is another retiree who likes going to the movies in the afternoon and prefers the middle back row, hubby is irritated that this person had the audacity to sit in *his* chair!

We enter the theatre with our popcorn and hubby looks up. His shoulders slump. I know what it means.

"There are three hundred other seats in here. Pick one!"

If someone sits too close to you in a theatre on your left, you lean on your right buttock and shoot them a glance, which is ridiculous, since you knew that people were going to be sitting near you, if not right beside you. You're in a movie theatre, after all.

It's the same scenario at the doctor's office. No one wants to sit in the corner, out of view of the doctor's door, in case they forget you're there, so the race is on to sit front and centre and try to look pathetic enough every time the nurse happens to glance your way.

Trying to find a seat in a restaurant can be as stressful as musical chairs. No one wants to sit in a chair when there is a plush banquet on the other side of the table. No one wants to sit in an aisle. No one wants to sit on the end. No one wants to sit near the bathroom. No one wants to sit near the front door in the winter. Everyone wants a booth. The worst is when you're the one sitting in the spot where they've shoved two tables together, because your plate is bound to be off-kilter. Who wants to sit at a table with wonky legs? And forget sitting next to the couple with four kids under the age of five.

Over your entire lifetime, how many arguments have you been in with your kids about this issue? Thousands.

"I don't want to sit in the back seat!" "I don't want to sit in the front seat!" "I don't want him sitting beside me!" "I don't want to sit!"

Finding someone else sitting in your seat on an airplane can give you a heart attack.

Ever go on a shuttle? You ask for the front seat and get it. Then the driver stops at a Tim Horton's in Antigonish for a ten-minute break. After everyone has been to the loo, bought a coffee and doughnut, and smoked a couple of cigarettes outside by the garbage bins, you walk back to find someone sitting in your front seat. Do you cause a scene, knowing you have to drive for three more hours to Halifax, or just let it go and mutter to yourself the rest of the way?

We are very possessive creatures. When something is ours, it's ours. Take church pews. Once you've claimed your spot, several generations of your family are forever destined to sit in that particular pew. And everyone in church knows it. If some hapless individual wanders in unknowingly and sits there, God help him.

Not that we can't share, but we need to be in the mood to share. Giving up your seat on a bus or a subway for a pregnant gal or elderly person is seen as a sweet gesture.

Anyone who doesn't share their seat in that case needs to sit in time out.

PARKING-LOT
OBSERVATIONS

"!"

P ARKING LOTS ARE AMAZING PLACES. IF ALIENS EVER LANDED, I'D DIRECT THEM TO the nearest one, to learn about humanity in a hurry.

There is a reason I specialize in parking-lot behaviour. Hubby is a "best deal" shopper. He'll go to seven separate stores to complete his grocery list. Naturally, I am the complete opposite and think he's foolish, so I usually don't venture out of the car when he pops into yet another retail outlet.

Hence, I spend a lot of time observing my fellow citizens, as they negotiate in and around several hundred cars, unpredictable people, and weapons of puny destruction, a.k.a. shopping carts.

First you have the vehicle pecking order. Men who drive big-ass trucks think they can park anywhere, and usually do, right in front of the store doors. Resist the urge to glare at them, because you don't know who's sitting that high up behind the tinted window. (I've been watching too much television.)

Then we have the teeny-tiny cars who park close to the top of the parking spot, and so trick other desperate drivers into thinking they have a great parking space, which they turn into, only to be sadly mistaken. You can actually see the swear words forming on the driver's mouth as they zoom away in frustration.

People who use up two parking spaces or park in accessible parking spots without a tag are at the bottom of the food chain.

Then we have the humans themselves. It takes some of them twenty minutes to actually get out of their car. These are usually young families with 2.8 kids in tow. They must first remove the huge Cadillac stroller from the trunk and fiddle with it. Dad is always in the middle of getting it ready when Mom comes over and impatiently interrupts. The thing obediently springs open and stands waiting for her next command. Then the struggle is on to get two kids out of the back seat with their puffy snowsuits on. Inevitably, the older child doesn't want his hat or mitts on and darts away, causing the parents to have a collective stroke. We then have Mom bend over and stick her finger in her child's face to warn them to never do that again. Dad usually picks up the kid, who is now howling into his shoulder. So much fun.

Perhaps the most frustrating scenario for drivers trying to manoeuvre through crowded lanes is the shopper who is oblivious to everyone around them. These are the people who walk in the centre of the lane at a snail's pace while four and then five cars line up behind them. We have several varieties of these creatures. First, there are the youngsters who have wires sticking out of their ears, and the little old ladies who know that at the age of eighty-five, they have earned the right to saunter wherever they damn well please. The ones we get really mad at are the middle-aged types who not only walk slowly, but zigzag across the lane several times before making it to the front door of the store. You think you're going to pass them, but no. They head you off like a meandering bison on the Canadian Prairies.

It's quite easy to identify the state of people's marriages just by seeing how they unload their bags. If a man does nothing but jump in the car, leaving a woman to empty the cart, deal with the kids, and put the cart back in the stall, he gives off a jerkish aroma. A man who pushes the cart, unpacks the cart into the trunk of the car, and holds the door open for his wife is swoon-worthy. (Please note that hubby is in this category.)

The ones I get a kick out of are the elderly men who are left in the driver's seats of their cars to wait for their wives. These women know they'll get things done a lot faster without their better halves. Besides, these guys have to babysit the "kid," a small, white, yappy dog, who sits happily in Dad's lap while they wait for the woman of the house.

But I'd really like to applaud the ladies out there who are smart enough to press the panic button on their key fobs so they can find their cars in an instant, instead of spending an hour trying to remember where they parked.

PEEK-A-BOO

"/"

THANKS TO THE INTERNET, YOU CAN FIND OUT WHAT'S WRONG WITH YOU IN A BIG, fat, hurry. Something you thought was nothing always turns out to have a name.

Apparently, I am prone to something called pareidolia. It sounds like something fungal, but it's the ability to find faces in random objects, which makes me fall in love with rocks, trees, floor tiles, toast, stains, and wallpaper.

Mostly, I can see cute faces, because that's what I gravitate to. If I spy something sinister, I will avoid it, which isn't easy when it's on the floor, right in front of the toilet. I'll find a nice face in the towel hanging up instead.

Faces are everywhere. On houses, fire hydrants, slippers, vegetables, old furniture, driftwood. Everywhere I look, I see something. There's an old bookcase by my desk. At eye level, the grain in the wood looks exactly like the Grinch when he smiles his evil smile.

One of my favourite children's books is *Bedtime for Frances* by Russell Hoban. Looking at the crack in the ceiling makes Frances think of something with a lot of skinny legs in the dark. I used to gaze at cracks in the ceiling in all the old houses we lived in when we were first married. Sometimes I saw a fox, Jed Clampett, or a gorilla. I've been known to stare at someone's sweater in a doctor's office because I'm positive Freddy Mercury is looking at me.

All the electric sockets in the house are my friends. They look worried and shocked, or on edge. Little innocent faces seeking comfort.

Now, I've never had any religious sightings, like the face of Jesus or the Virgin Mary on the bricks outside of a Tim Horton's, but I did see John Wayne on a potato once. I've also peeled quite a few carrots that were anatomically correct.

Surely, most people have varying degrees of this condition. To watch clouds go by is a favourite pastime. When we think we see something, we always tell someone else.

Facial recognition propels me to stalk elderly ladies who happen to look like my mother. Sometimes it isn't just the face. It may be the way they walk, so I get as close as I can, to just pretend for a minute that it's her.

One man came out of the liquor store while I was waiting in the grocery store parking lot, and his eyebrows and chin were exactly like my dad's. I wanted to get out of the car and hug him. You don't realize how much you miss your loved ones on a daily basis until you run into someone who has their characteristics.

We're always a blubbering mess when we see a dog that looks just like a dog we used to love. We insist on telling the owner the long, drawn-out story of our mutt while they grimace and just want to get on with their walkies.

When we watch movies like *WALL-E*, we immediately love the robot, because of his expressive binocular eyes. Same thing with *E.T.* When robots or machines have human characteristics, we treat them as if they are alive and have feelings.

Let's face it. We're all drawn to a pretty face. Which is why I have a piece of driftwood that looks exactly like a humpback whale. And most of us pick up rocks that have the shape of a heart.

Perhaps I look for faces in things because I'm so drawn to faces of every kind. I'm always looking for inspiration for characters in my books. Interesting faces are the best. Someone with a face full of wrinkles, or freckles, or who has huge ears or a long neck. Something that makes them stand out in the crowd.

Most people don't think they have beautiful faces, but they do.

SAD NOTES

"**!**"

I HAD A GREAT WEEK. LIFE IS SO EXCITING IN LOCKDOWN.

On Sunday, a squirrel flew into my face.

On Monday I wore a stupid bug jacket and got two nasty blackfly bites anyway, one on my ankle bone (don't you love to scratch that spot?) and one on the back of my hand that turned a nasty shade of red.

On Tuesday I had to make the world's biggest fruit salad, because hubby put two cantaloupes and honeydews in the downstairs fridge when he came home with the groceries, and I wasn't aware of it because I hate going down there, and I already had a cantaloupe and honeydew upstairs. And he bought two watermelons, even though I already have a half of one in the fridge, plus a pineapple, and two packages of blueberries as well.

"What is going on?!" I sputtered. "Only you and I live here, and you don't eat a lot of fruit."

"You like fruit."

"To a point! If I cut all this up, I might as well invite cruise-ship passengers over for breakfast."

On Wednesday I tried to stop wearing my wedding and engagement rings because I was washing my hands so much, my fingers were getting dried out and red and itchy. Here's a warning: don't bother. Taking off your wedding rings when you've been in a pandemic for over three months is not doable. The weight you've gained will prevent your rings from going anywhere. My twenty-minute struggle with olive oil and Vaseline counted as my aerobic exercise for the day.

Nothing happened on Thursday because there's so little to do here now. Unless you count fighting over the fact that hubby ate the last of the cashews.

On Friday night we watched *Peaky Blinders* in bed and it was an exercise in frustration.

"What the hell is he saying?'

"I don't know."

"Turn it up."

"Stop talking. Now I really don't know what he said."

"Why are they killing that guy?"

"How should I know?"

"Are these guys Irish, Scottish, or English? I can't tell. All they do is mumble."

On Saturday, I wrote this amazing piece.

Shit.

PIANO OR GUITAR?

"I"

THIS ACTUALLY HAPPENED.

It was two days after Christmas, on our way home to Cape Breton.

"Let's go look at that half-price piano keyboard before we head out."

"No."

"All you do is talk about taking piano lessons. Here's an opportunity to get a keyboard."

He was right. "Fine."

But I wasn't in a good mood, since I needed yet another root canal and we were both incubating the flu but wouldn't know it until the next day. The parking lot was a disaster. No one could get in or out because of the traffic. The store was even worse. It was packed solid with people coughing and sneezing and dragging hundred-inch televisions under their arms.

[Author's note: This was obviously not written in 2020.]

We went to the music section and found the keyboard. There was a young associate with long hair behind the counter, rubbing a guitar clean with a cloth. John went up to him and asked about the keyboard that was on sale. The kid said he had to find out if they had any more besides the floor model. He leisurely strolled to a glass-encased room where they had guitars hung up for people to try out. He rummaged around in there for a while and then came back out and went back behind the counter.

John asked if he found any.

"No. I'll look in the back."

Wasn't that what he was doing? Is there a back and then the real back? He shuffled off into the main part of the store. It was like he was moonwalking. How can someone be moving forward but seemingly backward at the same time? It took him three minutes to finally disappear.

"What is wrong with that kid?" I grumped. It was hot and stuffy, and I was in pain and annoyed to be standing there. All I wanted to do was sit down, but didn't dare on the flimsy metal bench in front of the keyboard.

Hubby can be amazingly patient in these situations, and he was unruffled, which ticked me off.

"This is stupid. Let's just go."

"Lesley, you have been talking about learning how to play the piano again, like your mom. I'd like you to be able to do it. Consider it your Christmas present."

When people are nice like that it's hard to remain grumpy, so I sighed and waited. And waited. And waited.

Finally, I spy Michael Jackson drifting our way. He's in no particular hurry, which strikes me as odd. When a sales associate is gone for a length of time, they usually hustle to get back to you to let you know they're working hard and they apologize for the delay.

"We don't have any more," he says.

The three of us look at the keyboard. "How old is this floor model?"

"Not sure. I'll find out."

And before we can object, he heads off into the bowels of the store again.

"Who is he talking to? Why does he have to keep going back there to find the answers?"

Hubby shrugs. I'm feeling so rotten at this point, I don't even smile when a kid walks up to the keyboard and flips a switch. The keyboard starts playing organ music with a flamenco beat. His father tells him to knock it off.

Finally, I see the sales guy coming our way again, but he stops to talk to another customer first. My temptation is to reach out and grab his name tag. He eventually returns.

"Don't know how old it is. But if you want it, it's the only one here. It's being discontinued."

"What do you think, Les? Do you want the floor model?"

All I can think of are the hundreds of germy kids who have fingered those keys in the last few months, so I make a face.

"I might be able to give you a discount," our helpful guy says. "Just a minute."

And he walks away to the glassed-in portion of the guitar room.

"What's he doing now?" I hiss.

He trudges back to the counter with a guitar and stays there, so we walk over to him.

"What's the verdict?" hubby asks him.

"You can have this guitar for ten percent off."

John and I look at each other, and then back at him.

"But we don't want a guitar." John points at the keyboard. "We're asking about that."

"Oh. Let me check."

And he shuffles off and disappears out back.

We stare at each other with our mouths open. Did that just happen?

"Okay, this is sign. Let's roll."

We left. I'm sure Michael Jackson never noticed.

THE WALMART SHUFFLE

"I"

WHEN YOU ARE A RETIRED COUPLE, THE NUMBER-ONE ADVENTURE OF THE WEEK IS your shopping trip. For some reason, both of you have to go. You can have your own adventures too. Hubby always manages to get in a trip to Home Depot, Canadian Tire, or Central Supplies without me, for which I am eternally grateful, and I always manage to leave the house without him for a hair appointment, pedicure, or massage, only because he wouldn't be caught dead at those places.

But inevitably, we both have to go to Walmart for supplies. And all is good, until we walk in the door. My first stop is always the washroom. While he collects the cart and makes a big deal about cleaning the handle with a towelette, I say, "I'll meet you at the veggie section."

"I have to go get kitty litter, Tums, and Tylenol first."

"Well, I have to find a cheap bra, so I'll go there and then meet you at the grapefruit stand."

We part company. And so begins the unfortunate saga.

After unsuccessfully finding the one lousy object I came in for, I wander over to WHERE I SAID I'D BE.

He's definitely not at the grapefruit stand, and after waiting there for what seems like forever (six and a half minutes), I move on, systematically marching down the one long aisle that looks into all the shorter food aisles to see if I can see him, starting in the veggie section and plodding along to the last aisle that contains the milk, yogurt, and cheese. There are at least a hundred retired men meandering the aisles, but not one of them belongs to me.

This situation would be remedied if we both had a cellphone, but we're cheap, so we share one, which is useless for finding your mate at a big box store. The law of averages suggest that I will find him eventually, but by the time that happens, I'm already planning our divorce. After another twenty minutes, I wonder how I'm going to tell the kids that I lost their father.

Maybe he fell and can't get up? But surely I'd run into him if that was the case. Did he meet an old friend in some obscure back aisle? Men are worse gossips than women, and they could stand there jawing all day, given half the chance. Just where the heck did he go? Back to the car? I hustle to the parking lot and promptly forget where we parked, so now I'm darting around trying not to look obvious. When I do eventually find the car, it's empty. It's not possible he's in that store! I've looked everywhere.

Should I go back and get the store involved? Do I really have to nerve to ask them to say over the intercom: "If Lesley Crewe's husband is still in the store, will he please come to the information desk before her head explodes?"

Better not chance it. He'd never forgive me. I end up shouting into the men's washroom.

"JOHN?"

Nothing.

"JOHN?"

"Yes, this is the john," a man replies.

Even in my heightened state, I thought that was really funny. I told him so.

"Thank you," says the voice.

My hair must have been on end, because the Walmart greeter is looking at me with concern. "Can I help you, ma'am?"

"I've lost my stupid husband!"

"It happens a lot."

"And are they ever found?"

"Unfortunately."

And who comes around the corner with a full cart but hubby, looking furious. "Where on earth have you been? I sat outside that women's change room for an hour."

He has the nerve to be mad at me?!

"John, I said I'd meet you by the grapefruit, and you weren't there."

"I waited by the grapefruit and you never showed up."

"If we had another phone, we wouldn't have to do this every time."

"I am not getting into a discussion about phones in public. Let's go. My feet are sore from running about this joint looking for you."

"My feet are sorer than yours." This is what it comes down to.

We sulk our way through the checkout and march to the car. After putting our seat belts on, he turns to me. "Did you get whatever you were looking for?"

"No. Did you get my grapefruit?"

"No."

"Why not?"

"I was too busy looking for you. Why didn't you get it?"

"You had the cart, mister!!"

STRANGER THINGS

"I"

I'M POSITIVE MY HUBBY HAS A LIST AS LONG AS YOUR ARM ABOUT THE WEIRD AND ridiculous things I do in the run of the day, but he's not a writer and he's not looking for material for a column. I am, and so today I'm going to discuss the nonsensical things that this man does in his daily life. And don't worry, he knows I'm doing this.

Every wife out there has her own particular index of her partner's wacky vices, which she normally brings up when a marital argument is not going her way. It's like Post-it Notes stuck to her brain for safekeeping. She never knows when she might need ammunition.

But it's not just irritating stuff. It's the funny stuff. Harmless and silly.

I was heading off to town one morning on a very windy day. As I backed the car out of the driveway and started to slowly drive up the laneway, I peeked at the house, and for a second, I thought I was hallucinating. The wooden rails along the front porch were all moving this way and that, like they got together in a frenzied attempt to wave me goodbye. The sight made me slam on the brakes, sure that I was having a stroke.

It turns out that hubby, in his infinite wisdom, had hammered out the bottom nail of each rail so he could shovel the snow off the front deck by just shoving it off the entire edge, all forty feet of it. Since I'm not the one shovelling it, I can't comment on this method, but I do know one thing. For someone who likes her pillows a certain way on the couch, it's very disturbing to come home and see three or four rails on the front deck leaning over sideways, as if they were drunk.

Speaking of pillows, if I accidentally put back John's water glasses the wrong way in the cupboard, he will instantly go out to the living room and mess up my pillows, just to remind me how irritating it is.

Since we live in the country, how we dress to go outside is an afterthought, but even I have some standards. One morning in the winter, hubby came in from feeding the birds and he had on the world's ugliest hat. A very thick knitted number that refuses to stay on properly and so slowly rides up his head until it's standing upright above his ears, shaped exactly like an eggplant. To top it off, underneath he had on his huge white earphones, the kind hip-hop DJ's wear, so he can listen to the BBC's *Danny Baker Show*. This image is burned in my brain.

There is a constant battle going on in this house with food. John is still trying to gain weight and I'm still trying to lose it. I've asked him to keep his goodies out of sight, so there are food caches all over this house. It's a good thing I don't clean too often, or I'd be finding surprise packages everywhere. But almost every single night, I go to the kitchen to get my one-point yogurt container out of the fridge and inevitably run into John sneaking upstairs with a bowl of peanut-butter-and-chocolate ice cream. It's like he knows! He says it's my fault for always being in the wrong place at the wrong time. He's a big creep-a-zoid for even having this kryptonite in the house.

He also has a big problem with my banana habits. Inevitably, I forget to take the sticker off the peel. This is a crime in his mind. He composts the fruit and veggie skins and says that having stickers show up in his compost the next year is akin to environmental disaster. I have come into the kitchen in the morning and there, on the table, is the sticker plastered on my placemat, and the offending banana skin has a message on it, written in ink: "TAKE OFF THE STICKER!!!" He actually wrote on a banana skin. Who does that?

But this man also picks up worms on our laneway so they won't be run over by a car. He doesn't throw them off to the side of the road. He figures out the best spot for worm condos and places them there.

How could you not fall in love with this maniac?

THE DIFFERENCE
BETWEEN
MEN AND WOMEN

" I "

T HIS IS A TOPIC THAT HAS BEEN DONE TO DEATH, BUT THAT'S NOT GOING TO STOP ME.
Men don't listen. The minute a woman opens her mouth, men look down and wonder who won the hockey game last night.

Women do listen, but they roll their eyes and put their hand on their hip throughout the explanation.

Men can't find anything. They need a woman to tell them that the thing they're looking for is five inches to their left.

Women can find everything. They've had a lot of practice, looking for stray socks, sniffing out joints in their teenager's bedroom, and rooting through junk drawers to find a twist-tie.

Men love to cook. They love throwing a steak on the barbeque, then sitting and drinking two beers until it's ready.

Women hate to cook. While hubby is "cooking" dinner on the barbeque, she's in the kitchen making potato salad, coleslaw, broccoli salad, fried onions and mushrooms, tea biscuits, and ambrosia for dessert.

Men hate shopping. Unless it involves wood or power tools.

Women love shopping. Unless it involves wood or power tools.

Men never put sunscreen on unless you shout at them, and then they still usually refuse.

Women will put sunscreen on their kids, the neighbour's kids, strangers, and the crossing guard. Even the dog isn't safe.

Men will only go to movies they like.

Women will go to any movie, even crappy sci-fi superhero stuff, because going to a movie is technically a date night, and when was the last time she had a date night?

Men can sleep through a home invasion.

A woman can hear her baby sneeze in their crib from downstairs in the laundry room, with the washer and dryer going.

Men have to be nagged into going to get their hair cut.

Women will go to the hairdressers if it's a Tuesday.

Men don't care what restaurant they go to.

Women don't care what restaurant they go to, as long as they get to pick it.

A man will order an extra-large pepperoni pizza for the whole family.

A woman will order an extra-large pizza, a quarter with pepperoni, a quarter with just cheese, a quarter with pineapple and chicken, and the other quarter a gluten-free vegetable, so everyone is happy.

Men can't understand why women love pillows so much. Pillows they aren't allowed to use.

Women can't understand why men don't get the "pillows on the bed" thing.

A man will post the recycling rules on the fridge. He will explain them to his family and lose his mind when a Tim Horton's cup finds its way into the paper blue bag. "This is garbage, people!!"

A woman tries to follow the rules, but if a piece of torn-up Ritz Cracker box lands in the plastic blue bag, she's not going to rummage through the bag to get it out, unlike some people.

Men like showers.

Women like bubble baths.

Men will wipe themselves dry with the dog towel.

Women keep the best towel in the house to themselves. It's usually in a secret hiding place.

A man will complain about a sore tooth.

A woman will make his dental appointment.

A man will say into the telephone, "Well, I don't know. You better ask your mother."

A woman will say into the telephone, "Oh God. Don't tell your father."

A man will put money in an envelope and not even write his kid's name on the envelope, and the kid thinks it's the best gift ever!

A woman will shop and hunt and search for the perfect gift and wrap it up beautifully. The rotten kid takes it back to the store because they don't like it. "I really like gift cards," they hint.

A man who says the kids can't have a cat is the one person in the family the cat loves.

A woman who let the kids have the cat in the first place is left to clean up the barf.

A man goes to Costco and buys a flat of corn chips.

A woman goes to Costco and buys a flat of toilet paper.

PICTURES

"I"

ALL MY LIFE I'VE HATED HAVING MY PICTURE TAKEN.
People who struggle with weight issues are particularly hard on themselves, but it's not just about wanting to look slimmer. I could be a size zero and I'd still hate it, because no matter what I do, no matter how hard I try, my face does not want to cooperate.

Every picture someone takes of me has me in mid-sneeze, or with my eyes squeezed shut, not to mention my mouth always hanging open, or with a lopsided grin, or worse, a gummy grimace. Then my chins multiply while I stare off into space or point at a crow. I can never sit still or stop talking long enough to say "Cheese." Just as the camera clicks, I'm muttering, "Oh my God, my hair!"

Nowadays, everyone and his dog knows how to pose for pictures, but I've never had the nerve to tilt my head coquettishly, or bat my eyelashes at a camera lens. It seems so phony and silly. The thought of pouting gives me the willies. So I guess I'll never take a good picture, because that's what it seems to take.

It must be an innate talent, because we all know that person who *always* take a great photo. They could be bungee jumping and their face is perfection as they leap into oblivion. How do they do it? It doesn't have to be someone gorgeous. Just someone who looks unfailingly great no matter where they are or what they're up to.

You have to envy perfect-picture pros. Let's face it. Pictures are all that's left of us when we leave this planet. Future family members will gaze at our faces and say, "I thought you said she was pretty."

Cameras on cellphones scare me. For some reason, I always have the camera facing me when I turn it on, and the sight of me staring down at the lens is horrifying. Every wrinkle, age spot, blemish, stray chin hair, and droopy eyelid is suddenly magnified a hundred times over. I've actually jumped back in fright.

Please remind me never to look over a cliff or the edge of a bed again.

And then every once in a while, like once every two decades, someone will capture you in an unguarded moment, and it's a wonderful picture. It makes you look so much better than you are. You can't quite believe it and you try to think up ways to show as many people as possible. You whip out your phone to take a picture of your meal at a restaurant. "This looks so fabulous! Doesn't this look fabulous?" You "accidentally" wipe your thumb across the screen as you pass it over.

"Wow! That's a great picture of you!"

You take back the phone as if you didn't know it was there. "This? Really? Do you think so?" (This is necessary, so they'll say it again.)

"You look amazing."

"Don't be silly." You grin like a mad fool before putting your phone away. When more friends join the table, you'll have to whip the phone out again to take a picture of them and "accidentally" wipe your thumb once more.

We've never been the type of people to have formal portraits done. On one occasion, I did broach the subject, and these were the replies: "Yuck, gross," "Not on your life," and "That's stupid."

So, we have only one formal picture of the four of us, taken during a York dungeon tour in jolly old England. Hubby is holding up a bloodied severed head, our son is gripping an axe and has it poised over his sister's neck while she leans above a wooden block, and I'm clutching a basket for her head to roll into.

It's charming. And explains so much about us as a family.

SHOES!

"I"

WHEN I WAS SIX YEARS OLD, MY MOTHER'S FRIEND MRS. YOKOHAMA GAVE ME A PAIR of brocade zōri sandals from Japan. They were my favourite thing in the whole world. I slid around the house, endlessly bowing to everyone, wishing with all my heart I could be Japanese. I'm happy to say I still have them, a little worse for wear but still beautiful in my eyes.

My next love affair with shoes happened when I was enrolled in tap dancing. Shiny black patent-leather shoes that you tied with a ribbon, with metal plates on the bottom to make as much noise as possible. "Shuffle-one, shuffle-two," over and over again. I was in heaven. My parents, not so much.

Then came the day we had to go to Browns Shoes in Montreal. This I loved because my last name was Brown, and I assumed I was related to these very wealthy and important people. A girl in school quickly set me straight and told the other girls milling around. That's probably why I hated the oxford shoes I had to wear with my school uniform.

But that was the only sour note, and it didn't last long. Then I moved to a new school that didn't require a specific uniform. It was like being freed from jail! I bought a pair of polka-dot sneakers to celebrate, but I must admit, my feet were sore by the end of the day. In hindsight, the oxfords were indestructible.

Then came high school in the seventies, with Dr. Scholl sandals. How I loved them. I'd clip-clop a mile to school in these things, my toes hanging on for dear life to the wooden sole by a strap of leather. They had no comfort whatsoever, but because they looked cool and annoyed my grandmother, I thought they were the bee's knees.

In university, I bought a pair of knee-high, soft, doe-brown leather lace-up boots that made my sister and her friends green with envy. They went perfectly with my jean skirt and black turtleneck. Not once did I ever pay for drinks when I wore that outfit. Ah, the good old days.

As a young married woman in the late seventies, if we were going out for the night, I'd wear Candies. Remember those? They were like a pair of Dr. Scholl's with very high heels. The kind I'd break my ankles in today.

And then came the parched period of my life. The kids arrived and I forgot I had feet. For twenty years, Birkenstocks schlepped my brood from pillar to post. Never bothered with running shoes; I didn't have time to lace them up.

Once I woke up and found myself alone again, I went to the shoe store and realized my feet were now as wide and flat as pancakes. Curses! Suddenly my love of shoes took a painful turn. It was impossible to find shoes that fit, so I'd cram my feet into anything, refusing to consider I might now need a size ten if I wanted something comfortable. I was in denial for a dozen years until our fateful trip to the British Isles.

Hubby had me climbing up every bloody castle in England, Scotland, and Wales. After an entire month of this, I realized that my right foot was completely and utterly numb. I could step on a tack and not feel a thing.

Every day he'd be fifty feet ahead of me, gesturing with his arm for me to hurry it up, while I limped with my bum foot over cobblestones. He had me running to catch trains, or humping luggage down six flights of stairs to the Underground at Piccadilly Circus. It never occurred to me to tell him to stuff it. That only happened when I turned sixty.

So now my feet are a real problem. I have a certified orthotist on speed dial. She made inserts for my feet and now I have to buy very, very expensive shoes in specialty stores to fit these inserts. If you're lucky, you can find something you like, but it's really depressing to buy a pair of shoes that are size 42 DD.

My feet now match my boobs.

TIME SAVERS

"I"

DON'T YOU JUST LOVE THE GIZMOS THAT SOCIETY COMES UP WITH TO SAVE YOU GOBS of time? There's a huge industry out there that spends every minute of the day devising devices to make our lives easier.

But what they seem to forget is that actual human beings have to use them. And humans are often stressed and panic-stricken, through no fault of their own. They often get that way because of these fantastic time savers.

Like key fobs.

The fact is, I didn't even know what a fob was until the man who sold us our car passed me a fat, pear-shaped thingy that you press to open the door. Apparently, these weird things cost hundreds of dollars. This makes me nervous right off the bat. What's wrong with just having a key? A key I understand. A fob is heavier and takes up more space in your hand, your pocket, and your purse.

And it gets really irritating when I try to open my car with it and it doesn't work. This is when panic strikes. Press, press, press, and press. Nothing. Oh my God. How am I going to get home? Oh! Phew. There's another fob in my purse. And press.

Nothing.

Now I'm alone in a parking lot with heavy plastic bags hanging off me. A cloudburst appears directly over my head and the sky opens. I'm drenched and swearing. If I had a key, I could open the door and get in out of the weather. I start to run back to the store and accidentally hit the fob. There's a click behind me. The door opened. I'm thirty feet away, but it works.

223

Once I'm home I tell hubby and he shows me that there is a key in the fob if I need to use it. "Why didn't you tell me that before? And if they go to that much trouble, why not just have a key?"

He tries to teach me how to access the key. Nope. Not happening. He can. Not me.

So now I have to be three hundred feet from my car to have the fob work. If I stand right beside the car, it doesn't budge. If you see me forever running around parking lots pointing that damn fob over my head or behind my back, trying to get the blasted thing to work, just ignore it.

This is not saving time or my sanity.

Then we have the dream of self-serve checkouts. Never has anything gone right in this area. It takes me ten minutes to read all the instructions. It takes another ten minutes to figure out why the machine doesn't like me. Carefully, I place the stuff in the bag on the scale like it told me to, but it insists I didn't. The machine is basically calling me a liar.

It's time to try and find the one person responsible for this hellish part of the store, but she is madly running from machine to machine, helping other people who are being called liars by their checkouts.

Not once have I ever put my card in the right spot, or found where the receipt is supposed to come out. I'd never put cash in there, in case it doesn't give me change. It's just altogether too stressful. And even when I eventually look pathetic enough for an employee to notice me, it's like they don't believe me when I say I did put the item in the bag.

"You have to put the item in the bag."

"I did put the item in the bag."

"If you did, it would let you continue, but right now it's stopped."

"Yes, I realize it's stopped, but it shouldn't have stopped, because I put the item in the bag."

She's thinking I'm a useless human being, but I'm just a poor housewife trying to get home with my cheese slices, vanilla yogurt, and grapefruit.

The girl cancels whatever I've been doing for the last half an hour and re-enters the produce. It works beautifully for her. She gives me a big smile. I grimace and hurry away, shouting, "Thank you so much."

Now to head out to the parking lot, but naturally I forget about the fob and when I click it as I near the car, it refuses to work. The door stays locked, so I have to walk back to the entrance and point again. It opens.

So far, I have wasted forty minutes trying to get in and out of Superstore.

SNIPPETS

"I"

I BOUGHT A NEWFANGLED CURLING IRON. A BIG MOTHER WITH NO COVERING. IT'S A giant phallic piece of molten lava. A big father.

My inner wrists, arms, knuckles, and forehead are now scarred for life as I try to navigate twisting my hair with my bare fingers around a *Star Wars* sabre that's hot enough to broil steak.

No one is going to look at my hair with all these brown burn marks all over me. I wore long sleeves last night at my Zoom reading, in case the audience became concerned.

I'M SO CROSS! I LOST my little gold bracelet this morning. I just found the darn thing two months ago while cleaning out my so-called jewelry box. I'd forgotten all about it and was delighted to see it again. The gold looked really nice against my leathered rawhide wrist, which is what happens to old skin when you sit on a beach for two months.

We were in the canoe paddling and I suddenly looked down and there was my stupid wrist...without a speck of gold on it.

"Oh my God! My bracelet fell off!"

"Where?" says the bright man behind me.

"Where? I'm assuming in MIRA BAY!!! I don't believe this!"

"You shouldn't have worn it out on the water."

In my head, I turn around and smack the bright man in the face with my paddle. It's politically incorrect to haul off and hit someone in the mouth with a piece of wood, but honestly. Does he really think making that kind of comment is helpful? Since I'd already thought the same damn thing a moment earlier? I didn't need to hear it said out loud.

I'm pouting like a two-year-old. It's like 2020 just won't quit.

SOMETHING ELSE TO GRIPE ABOUT.

We inherited our son's seven-pound cat. She's as light as a feather. But the second I sort of shut the door to our bedroom at night to drown out the living room television, she inevitably takes her tiny paw and slams the door wide open to come in, like she's friggin' John Wayne arriving at a saloon in the Old West.

BANG!!

"For the love of God! How do you do that?"

I wonder if I can sign her up for boxing lessons.

THIS JUST HAPPENED. I got a call from a hardware store.

"Hello?"

"Hi. Just to tell you that your sledgehammer arrived."

"Err..."

I hold the phone to my chest. "John? Did you order a sledgehammer? "

"Yes."

I put the phone back to my ear. "Fine. Thank you dear," I say to the young voice and hang up.

If you never hear from me again, please give this information to the police.

A FRIEND REMINDED ME OF something that happened years ago.

My little daughter was sitting between a friend of mine and her grandmother on the couch. She was about three. She was looking at their hands.

"Why are your hands smooth and your hands wrinkly?"

Her grandmother smiled. "My hands are wrinkly because I was a nurse and I had to wash them with very harsh soap."

Sarah looked up at her innocently. "Did you have to wash your neck too?"

I RECEIVED MY BEST CHRISTMAS present ever when I was on a Zoom call with my little granddaughter, Gia, who turned eleven months old yesterday. My face appeared on the screen and she gave me a big drooly grin and cried out, "Harmi!"

Her mother speaks Korean to her all the time and the word for grandmother is *Harmoni*. I tell Gia I'm her Grammie, so Harmi is what she came up with!!! I was so delighted I almost cried and she said it three times, but of course hubby gets in on it and keeps yelling "Say Grandad!" to her, but all she does is stick her tongue out and make babbling noises because that's what he does to her all the time.

It's just magic.

HARMI'S FIRST BIRTHDAY GIFT

"**/**"

B UYING A GIFT FOR GIA'S FIRST BIRTHDAY PARTY IS AS EXCITING AS LEARNING MY
novel *The Spoon Stealer* made the top ten bestsellers list for fiction in
Canada three times in the fall of 2020. (I'm getting so good at self-promotion.)

Her grandfather, who at this point is called Dad-Dad, came up with
a great idea and bought her a wagon, which she'll need in the spring once
she's worn out the sled we bought her for Christmas. It's a two-seater, for
Gia and a friend, or perhaps a baby brother or sister?? But I can't go there.
My happiness dial would break.

Gia's Omma (Mommy) tells me she has enough clothes and toys at the
moment. So, what should I do? Her book collection in Korean and English
is already out of control.

Maybe a dolly?

Old-fashioned, but who cares? It doesn't mean she won't grow up to be
an astronaut. It's just something soft to hug. And learning to hug is important for our mental health. We missed that loving gesture the most in 2020.

So, I traipse to a few stores with my mask on and look for dollies.

Unbelievably, the only thing I see are Barbies and dolls that look like
the members of the band Pussycat Dolls, in full make-up and sexy clothes,
with enormous eyes and lips.

Every atom of my body vibrates in disgust.

Where are the baby dolls of my youth? Are they that scarce that you must hunt them down in specialty stores? There are a few tears shed at the thought that I'll never find a baby bottle with the milk that disappears when you tip it. Gosh, I loved that thing when I was a little girl. Although these days I'd probably find it on Amazon.

Discouraged, I head home for the day and then remember one more store, but if there's a lineup, I'm leaving. The longest I'll stay in a mall is about fifteen minutes, and that's not because of COVID-19, I've just always hated malls.

Rounding a corner of the toy section I look down at the bottom shelf by some miracle, and hidden away at the back is a Danish design wooden doll carriage painted lavender. It's beyond adorable and the perfect size for my blueberry. I grab it so fast, the woman behind me makes a face. I think. I can't know for sure because of her mask.

"Sorry. It's for my granddaughter's first birthday party."

She turns away and says nothing.

That's okay. She can't spoil this moment.

But then I remember I need a doll to put in the baby carriage and my heart sinks. Until I step around another corner and there is a wee cuddly doll with a cloth body and soft plastic face and hands. She's got a sweet smile and small, bright marble eyes, wearing a sleeping cap and a onesie. Can it be true?

When I pull into the driveway, Dad-Dad is soaked to the skin, shovelling watery snow.

"Guess what I got?!" I shout excitedly. "Gia's birthday present!"

"I thought we got her the wagon."

"We did. And this!" I pull out the little carriage and the doll from the back seat. "Can you believe it?! I'm so happy!"

He gives me a grin. "That is pretty cute."

A highlight of my life, for sure.

Unless Gia turns out like her Gomo (Auntie Sarah), and hates dolls with a passion and throws them under the bed, never to be seen again.

THE LIGHT HAS GONE OUT

"I"

T HE LAST OF THE THREE AMIGOS HAS LEFT US, AND THE HOUSE IS EXCRUCIATINGLY empty.

The presence of Pip's absence is everywhere, and we can't escape it. Now we can close the door to the basement because he's not going down there to use the kitty litter. Now we can leave the door open when we bring in groceries, because he's not going to escape to the great outdoors. There's no water dish, there are no cat dishes, there's no medicine on the counter. His favourite toy is now wrapped around the little wooden box that contains his ashes, and that is beside me as I type, a very poor substitute for the lovely, heavy, furry body that would drape himself over my arm as I sat writing my words.

When the kids left home, our dog, Harry, and his brother cats, Neo and Pip, cheered us up when the house was quiet. These three shared this space. We met each other at all hours, when one of us couldn't sleep. They witnessed so much laughter and so many tears. People who think that pets don't speak to you don't notice very much; pets have the best advice ever. They stay close, they listen, they nuzzle, and they look at you when you're not ready for the world to see your face. They see the real you, and love you anyway.

All of us who adore our cats or dogs or fish or rabbits or turtles or lions and tigers know that someday we will lose them, but we stay brave and bring them into our lives anyway. We spend our years together, deliberately not thinking of the day they will leave us. Because if you did, you'd go crazy.

And hubby and I are going crazy.

Yes, he was ill, he was fifteen, he had a good life and a good run, and he was lucky in a lot of ways, but we weren't ready. It happened so fast, and while we were away from home there was a panicked trip to a veterinary hospital we'd never been to, and suddenly it was obvious that this was it. What? Today? Now? But it's not possible. It's early in the morning and we're stuck in traffic and what is going on?

And when the lovely people who love animals look at you and ask you what you want to do, you look at them, knowing they are willing you to do the right thing and stop thinking of yourself and do what's right for Pip. And you want to take him in your arms, in the towel he's wrapped in, and run out of there and not look back, but you know that's not fair and he deserves to be cared for, especially now.

The lovely people offered water, Kleenex, a quiet, dark room, and time for the three of us to be together.

No one hurried us out of there. It was a long, private goodbye before we tucked him up and left him with the lovely people.

His ashes wouldn't be ready by the time we had to leave for home, and the thought of leaving him in Halifax and driving home without him was heartbreaking. How were we going to go home without him? All his things were where he left them.

We finally had to leave Halifax, and were on the highway to start our lonely journey when my cellphone rang. The lovely people said that Pip was ready to come home with us, earlier than expected. We immediately turned around and headed back into the city.

They handed us a little brown bag, with a light-coloured box with Pip's ashes inside, his name engraved on the top. There was also a clay medallion with his paw print pressed into it and a small plastic bag with some of his fur. We cried in their Quinpool parking lot. They must see that too often.

I held his little box against my heart all the way home.

It's where he belongs.

TELLING THE BEES

"I"

SOMETIMES YOU READ SOMETHING THAT INSTANTLY GIVES YOU PAUSE. One morning, I was drinking coffee in my pyjamas, browsing down my Facebook page, more out of habit than interest, when I came upon a marvellous little article from an obscure website, posted by a writer I met at a recent literary festival. Now, I love writers, because they are endlessly nosy about life, and they find the most incredible stories or even tidbits of information about the world and post them on their sites for the rest of us to enjoy.

This one took my breath away. It was about a tradition called "telling the bees."

In rural Britain and throughout Europe, it was customary for families to tell their bees of important family events. If there was a death in the family, someone had to go out to the hives to tell the bees of this terrible loss, because if they did not, calamity might befall the hive, like the bees leaving, or not producing honey, or even dying. Often, people would drape black cloth on the hives for good measure.

But not only death was reported. All important family matters were told to the bees. Special events such as births, marriages, or even journeys that resulted in people's absences for long periods of time. Newlyweds were encouraged to introduce themselves to the bees or their married life could be miserable, and sometimes the hives were decorated for this special day and pieces of wedding cake left outside for the bees.

They say this tradition has origins in Celtic mythology, as the bee is thought to be a link between our world and the spirit world. They say if you want to send a message to a loved one who has died, just whisper it to a bee and they will take it to them. This gives me incredible comfort, somehow.

Certainly, the intimate relationship between bees and their keepers is well known, but ultimately bees are essential to all of humanity and our survival. Seventy of the top one hundred crop species that feed ninety percent of our human population rely on bees for pollination, and without them, plants, as well at the animals who eat those plants, would cease to exist, so our connection to these tiny, precious creatures isn't only whimsical.

And while "telling the bees" sounds like a charming forgotten fairy tale in today's modern world, it gave me the shivers when I read about it, because of something my daughter-in-law told me recently.

Her Korean grandfather kept bees all his life and loved them very much. One sad day, he died, and the next morning, when the family went out to the hives, all the bees were gone.

They never did return.

How does one explain that? I'd like to think that perhaps they couldn't bear for him to leave, and so they accompanied him on his journey to the next life.

Who can say? Perhaps this quaint tradition is more than it seems. Nature is a mysterious and wondrous thing and I'm thankful that we can never know the whole truth of it, or explain it away. Bees can keep their secrets.

But I know the next time I see a fat, pollen-laden, fuzzy honeybee drunkenly hovering over the garden flowers, I'll not only tell her what's going on at our house, I'll thank her profusely for being such a perfect busy bee.

THE POWER OF FAMILY

"I"

TODAY A BEAUTIFUL WOMAN (WHO TOLD ME IT WAS HER EIGHTIETH BIRTHDAY), came up to me and said she knew my grandmother and that "She was such a lovely lady, so kind and sweet to us girls."

My eyes welled up with tears instantly. My grandmother was born 121 years ago. She's been gone for 34 years. I didn't expect to run into someone who actually knew her on this ordinary Thursday morning.

This dear woman gave me such a gift. The gift of missing my grandmother. The gift of longing for her, remembering her touch, her scent, her voice, and how she was a lovely lady, and how she would have been kind and sweet to young girls all those years ago, as she always was to us.

And it struck me that our lost loved ones are so close to the surface in our everyday lives. We get used to missing them after many years, and that reality becomes almost a backdrop, but bam...come face-to-face with someone else who talked to your grandmother and suddenly you want to take this woman in your arms and say, "Tell me everything you remember! What was she doing on that day? How did she look? What was she wearing?"

I missed the ache of losing her. And when that pain comes rushing in, so does her spirit, which is so welcome.

To say I'm envious of women my age who still have their mothers is an understatement. When it becomes too much and I need my mom, I'll take her perfume bottle and open it. There she is.

Lately, if I meet a woman named Bernice on one of my book tours, instantly I get up and hug her. Mom was a kindergarten teacher, and whenever I hear the word *kindergarten*, my heart does a tiny dance.

A few years ago, a car pulled up to my friend's bungalow. It was her friend, taking her elderly father out for a drive to the places he remembered in his youth. He couldn't get out of the car, so we shook his hand through the car window. He asked who I belonged to and I told him my grandfather, Kenzie, owned Shaw and Macdonald Machine Shop in Glace Bay, and he said he knew my grandfather very well.

I didn't let go of his hand, and he let me hold it the whole time we were talking. It was my grandfather's hand I was holding, reassuring me that he wasn't very far away, even though I lost him when I was twelve.

Memories are powerful, and to be able to mine someone else's memories of your loved ones is astonishing. Human beings are connected to each other, and if they have stories of the people you loved, you want to hear them. You need to hear them.

The lady who knew my grandmother told me she read my novel *Kin*, which is the story of my family. She said it made her very happy because she knew all the people in it, but she especially loved that I included my grandmother's lemon-meringue pie recipe, because she knew that my grandmother, Abbie, was a marvellous baker. She actually made that pie from the recipe in the back of my book, and it thrills me to know that she did. I don't know why. It just does. Possibly because the thought of someone eating that pie brings Grammie back to life again.

All I have to do is listen to the first six notes of Claude Debussy's "Clair de lune," and my dad is in the room with me. He's right there, playing the piano.

Those we've loved and lost are always right here, closer than we think. It's just a wondrous surprise to be reminded of that every so often.

FOREVER

"I"

I WANT TO TELL YOU ABOUT A MOMENT, GONE BEFORE I WAS ABLE TO GATHER A THREAD of thought. But once you know, its presence never leaves. It winds around you as mist, a wind that swirls, unseen but always felt. It only comes to you after losing someone you deeply love.

We lost our little boy, Joshua MacKenzie. A nurse told me she liked the way his name looked on a piece of paper. I have been staring at it carved in granite for ten thousand days.

The night Joshua died, I left this place. I went with him, carrying him into the universe myself. When I returned, pieces of my exploded heart lay all over the hospital floor. I tried to gather them up but couldn't. My breast milk dripped down the drain of a public washroom sink because my baby didn't need it any more. My body cried for me.

This is falling over the edge of the earth.

No mother should ever know what it feels like to leave her baby in the rain.

In school we learned that when ancient Hawaiians grieved for the people they loved, they climbed the sea cliffs and smashed their teeth against the rocks. They poked their eyes out with sticks. I used to wonder why someone would do such a thing.

They do it to let the pain out.

I wanted to be with Joshua. It would have been so much easier to die. The only reason I didn't was a four-year-old boy who said he would grow up to be Superman and save his brother.

Somehow we lived through that long lonely winter. Spring came and then summer. Early one morning, Paul wanted to be with his baby brother. We went to the cemetery and sat on the grass beside Joshua's grave. The sky was a beautiful clear blue, with glorious white clouds that rose so high they looked endless.

Paul was content. He sat on my lap and we listened to the brook dancing its way to the ocean. Birds and chipmunks greeted us as they always did. We saw butterflies and bugs, ants and even a grasshopper. The two huge fir trees on either side of Joshua's stone gave us shade from the bright sun.

I felt a flutter, as soft as silk. My girl let me know she was there too. I looked up between those towering trees and the sky split open. I had an unborn child, a living child, and a dead child. And they were all with me. Whether or not I could hold him, whether or not I could see her. They would stay with me in this world, the world before, and the world after.

I didn't lose Joshua. He lives with me every day, as surely as his brother and sister. Paul and Sarah are held in the circle of my arms. Joshua lies in his garden, in the circle of the earth, under a canopy of stars.

THE SPOON STEALER

"**I**"

IT MUST BE OBVIOUS BY NOW THAT FAMILY MEANS THE WORLD TO ME. AND I DIDN'T need the catastrophic year 2020 dropping out of the sky to remind me of that. It was drummed into my head from a very early age.

"Family is everything," my mother would say.

She would say that. She nearly died having me after contracting endocarditis, in addition to her rheumatic heart, and I added to the drama by nearly dying of pneumonia. My father was actually told I was dead, and then they came in to say "Oh sorry, wrong Mr. Brown, you have a boy." Just as he was crying with relief, they popped back round to say "Oops, it's a girl."

"Is there a grandmother in this picture?!" the doctor shouted at my dad. "Your wife must be on complete bedrest for six months."

Fortunately, there was a wonderful grandmother, Abbie, in Glace Bay, and she flew into Montreal with her Grammie cape on and saved the day. Mom says I was a scrawny chicken when she kissed me goodbye from her hospital bed, and when Super Grammie flew back with me six months later, I was a baby Buddha.

When Mom got her hands on me again, she never let go.

Having four babies myself and losing two of them, one to a miscarriage and the other to sudden infant death syndrome, was more than enough to convince me that nothing else in life matters.

Nothing.

And so, I always write about families.

But this last novel of mine, *The Spoon Stealer*, has become something more to me. It is about families, and mine in particular, but how it came to

239

be and when it arrived on the scene is bigger than me. And I am convinced that the power of family is not just about the people we live with in our lifetime, but our kin who came before us. They are living and breathing in your life too. How else could this have happened?

In October 2019, the thought of another novel kept swirling around me. The publishers weren't asking for one. My first non-fiction book, *Are You Kidding Me?!*, was out that fall, but I kept seeing this elderly Mary Poppins–type character named Emmeline flit in and out of my dreams, and knew I wanted her for something, but what? What should she do?

And then I kept going back to a story I knew only vaguely. That both my Grampy's brothers died in the First World War. Jack was in the navy and he drowned, and the other brother was gassed in France. I didn't know his name.

And it might have been my imagination, but I thought there was a story of my Grampy's sister Margaret going overseas to be with her brother, who was taken to a hospital in England, but he died the night before she got there.

I called our only remaining elderly relative to ask her and she confirmed it, but she didn't know very much more.

The idea of a young woman from Glace Bay travelling alone across the ocean to be with her big brother during the war was like something out of a movie. That's what I would use for Emmeline. That would be her storyline. How fantastic! Not that I would base the entire novel on it, but you need a jumping-off point, and this was the perfect scenario. And the fact that it was based on my own history just added to my glee.

But I was under a deadline. If I wanted this book written, I was going to have to do it before my first grandchild was born, because the minute that happened, my focus was going to be shot! Who cares about writing a novel when there's a perfect little blueberry in your life??

She was due January 24, 2020.

So, I started on Monday, November 18, 2019. The only reason I know this is because I wrote it in my diary: *Started The Spoonful—Emmeline—like the first page.*

But my problem was that I didn't know enough. Writing fiction is one thing, but I knew this was based on real facts and I wanted to get them right, even if no one would know the difference, so when I'd stop writing for the night, I'd look through old papers and boxes of pictures and files, my mother's notes, and the family Bible.

And I found what I was looking for. It was here all along.

I finished *The Spoon Stealer* on January 15, 2020. Gia Elizabeth was born on January 19, 2020.

And then the pandemic hit. When I wrote that book, I had no idea a pandemic was on the horizon, but when it did come crashing into our lives, I shivered.

What I learned about my grandfather's siblings was that the oldest brother, Coll Macdonald, who was gassed in France, didn't die during the war. He died in March 1919. His brother Jack (John Angus) drowned at the age of thirty in a freak accident in Liverpool, England, in December 1919. He was a lieutenant commander in the US Navy.

Margaret did travel overseas to try and get to her brother Coll, not during the war like I first imagined, but during the pandemic of 1919, when 20 to 50 million people lost their lives. And I know this because I found a letter Jack wrote to their sister Bay in August 1919, four months before he died, saying how he saw Margaret in England and how they went to Collie's grave. I have that letter, written one hundred years ago, describing the scene that I wrote about in *The Spoon Stealer*. A copy of that particular letter made its way into my hands. I've had it here for over twenty years, since my mother died, but I never knew I had it.

Suddenly my grandfather Kenzie's brothers and sisters came rushing back into my life. To read Jack's letter at the back of the book will have you in tears, because he was obviously charming and funny and had so much to live for.

And dear, sweet Margaret, travelling across the ocean at a time when danger lurked everywhere. I was afraid to go Christmas shopping because of COVID-19, and she battled her way across the Atlantic to be with a beloved brother, only to miss him by one day.

Why did I write this story when I did? Why did it come to me at this particular moment in my life? When another pandemic was crawling over the earth, unbeknownst to me.

To let me know that my family has been through this before. They came back to remind me that life goes on for all of us. We are not the only generation who have lived and died during these same circumstances.

So, when I get fed up from time to time with worrying about bubbles and masks and staying close to home and not seeing my granddaughter, I'll think about Margaret and Jack and Coll and know I come from stern stuff. I come from good people.

They came back to remind me when I needed them to.

That's what families do.

NOSY PARKER

"I"

WROTE A NOVEL IN A MONTH.

Thursday, February 4, 2021, to Thursday, March 4, 2021.

I have to write that down so I can believe it myself. It wasn't my intention to write a novel in thirty days, but it was my intention to dedicate a book to my father, the writer.

Nosy Parker is my fourteenth book. I'd written *The Spoon Stealer* the year before and the book *I Kid You Not!* you now hold in your hands. The publishers and I floated around the idea of writing a prequel to *The Spoon Stealer*, but my editor, Penelope, asked me, "Is it singing to you?"

The answer was no.

I told her that my next book would have to be dedicated to my father, since he was a writer and I couldn't figure out why I hadn't done it yet. My guilt about it loomed over me. But now I know why.

I was saving his dedication for this book.

It takes place in Montreal from April 1967 to September 1968. Because it just had to. My father and Montreal are inseparable.

My intention was not to write about my father's life. I have lived my father's life, so I didn't want to recreate it. Some of our memories rose to the surface, which I included, but it is a work of fiction. However, his essence is all over every page, as surely as if he'd walked in the room, with the scent of his aftershave and pipe tobacco lingering there.

I was halfway through the novel when I remembered that he used to call me Princess. It came to me in a dream. When I wasn't writing the novel in my study day after day, I was writing it in my sleep. Somewhere deep down, I knew he called me Princess, but I'd lost that memory. He's been gone so many years, and he didn't speak coherently for eight years, and then not at all before he died of Alzheimer's, so I'd forgotten the way it sounded when he said it.

The day after I finished the novel, my dear friend called and I told her how I was gobsmacked that I'd written this little book in thirty days and she said, "You know who I'm happy for? Your dad. He helped you write this book. There's no other explanation."

I went for a walk when I wrote the final word, and it was cold. Really cold. I hadn't been outside in a month, so I enjoyed this blast of crisp air, to clear my brain of its dizziness. You can't sit at a computer for twelve-hour days and not have it take a toll. And my brain felt fried.

I watched a flock of geese move across the sandbar and I cried and cried and cried for my father. I hadn't done that in a long time. It's always been much easier to cry for my mother, to miss my mother. But I'm going to miss him. I'm going to miss him so much. That's when I knew he was with me this entire time, because now that the book is done, he's going leave me once more.

But it won't be so easy for him to disappear, because now I have him at my fingertips.

He's in my novel *Nosy Parker*, coming in July 2022, about a twelve-year-old girl named Audrey Parker, who thinks she's a spy.

If you'd like to meet my dad, that's where you'll find him.